Contents

Introduction

'Never pray in a room without windows' is a profound insight from the Talmud. We do not pray to escape the world. We pray to become co-creators of the future – a future at peace with an ever-changing reality; a future rooted in hope; a future that is authentic; a future that is real.

The poet Rainer Maria Rilke, in 'God Speaks to Each of Us', writes:

God speaks to each of us before we are ...
Let it all happen to you: beauty and dread ...
Near here is the land
That they call Life.
You'll know when you arrive
By how real it is.

A Little Bit of Healing is an attempt to bring both reality and hope together in a helpful way. This is a selection from my many articles and broadcasts between 2007 and 2010.It has been a devastating time for Catholics as many struggle to hang unto what little faith they have left.

Trust has been destroyed by a succession of horrendous scandals. The Ryan and Murphy reports, which we accept as honest and truthful, have shown that our institutions, particularly in the Catholic Church, were built on sandy foundations critically weakened by hypocrisy.

Church leaders in dioceses and religious congregations deliberately covered up the evil abuse of children so that their power structures would be protected. They deemed the survival of institutions to be more important then the protection of children

Deep-seated anger is the only healthy reaction to this utter betrayal of everything Jesus Christ stood for. Yet unless we deal with anger, it will destroy us.

The sections of this book are compiled to help the reader re-

Brian D'Arcy CP

A Little Bit of Healing

the columba press

First edition, 2010, published by
the columba press
55A Spruce Avenue, Stillorgan Industrial Park,
Blackrock, Co Dublin

Cover by Bill Bolger
Cover photo by Pat Lunny
Origination by The Columba Press
Printed in Ireland by
Colour Books Ltd, Dublin

ISBN 978 1 85607 688 3

flect on the present state of religious belief and practice in Ireland in a way that might lead to peace and healing.

I begin in a comforting way by looking at the heroic lives of brave leaders who, by authentic living, overcame injustice. Next comes the hard graft of wading through some of the awful events which have caused a crisis in the Catholic Church as damaging as that which led to the Reformation. This will not be easy reading. However, the scandals, and the anger they invoke, cannot be glossed over. C. S. Lewis wrote: 'The prayer before all prayer is: May it be the real I who speaks. May it be the real Thou that I speak to.'

Healing is a slow organic process. It is a journey each of us must bravely launch out on; otherwise we choose to imprison ourselves in the dark vaults of despair. Hopefully, we can be brave enough to bring healing to *our wounded church* and, with God's grace, healing to *our wounded world*. In short, healing requires a number of steps:

Step one is a time for reflection, openness and perspective. We should acknowledge the positives (Part One).

Step two on the healing journey is facing the causes of the hurt as honestly and as objectively as possible (Part Two).

Step three requires us to sift through what can be changed and accept what cannot (Part Three).

Step four is realistically looking to the future with courage and hope. Healing demands that we give up hope of a perfect past so that we can have a better future (Part Four).

I take courage from Mary Oliver' poem:

One day you finally knew
what you had to do, and began
though the voices around you
kept shouting
their bad advice –
… But little by little,
as you left their voices behind
the stars began to burn
through the sheets of clouds,

and there was a new voice
which you slowly
recognised as your own,
and kept you company
as you strode deeper and deeper
into the world
determined to do
the only thing you could do –
determined to save
the only life you could save. (*The Journey*)

Denis Bradley, in his article 'Can the Church Reform?' (*Doctrine and Life*, July/August 2010) reminds us that 'long before any church came into being, this same God was dispensing his love and his grace and his salvation …' He goes on to highlight the damage which silence does when we are called by God publicly to search for truth, for hope and for healing. He distrusts cowardly silence. No matter how reticent we may be, we don't have a choice – we are duty bound to search for truth and to speak with integrity:

> Bishops and priests who say little or nothing from their pulpits or in their local media. Bishops who address the issue of abuse and the procedures that are being put in place but who say little or nothing in favour of or in opposition to reform … Silence from clerical academics who have views that should be heard but keep them to themselves. Silence from those who know that the obsequious obedience to Rome is making it difficult if not impossible for the Irish church to construct a roadmap out of the present mess but are too cautious or afraid to express their opinion. Silence from those who know that healthy debate is the very least that is needed but who fail to engage. Silence from those who fear that change for the sake of change can lead to greater chaos and hurt but who are too timid to stand up for their views. Silence may be golden but at a time when many good and faithful people feel hurt and disillusioned, silence could be a further act of betrayal.

I have tried not to be hurtful to individuals and have omitted many articles which might have been too critical. However, if I do hurt any individual, I apologise in advance.

I have prayed endless hours about the contents and will continue to do so. I have given my entire life to the Catholic Church and thank God every day that I am still able to serve as a priest. I believe with all my heart that Christ will not abandon his church, and I also believe that we have to endure the passion of many deaths before new life is possible.

I just hope that the lost and the lonely and the confused and the disillusioned will find some words for feelings too sacred to reveal.

The best way to read *A Little Bit of Healing* will be in short extracts. Let the words lead you to reflect on your own thoughts. You will not find all the answers; you may, however, find some helpful questions. As you read, trust your own judgement, recognise your own goodness; pray for healing and guidance; don't give up on God's goodness; don't run too easily from the priceless gift of faith itself, the value of a community of believers and, of course, the Eucharist. Claim ownership of your church. Most of all, don't confuse a dysfunctional clericalism (priests make up 3% of the church) with the real church.

I hope you enjoy this book – the pleasant, the controversial and the spiritual. If you agree with some of what I suggest, well and good. If you don't, take courage and come up with something better.

Lastly, thanks to all at The Columba Press for their guidance in selecting and editing this collection. I appreciate the help of many honest friends for challenging me to be a helpful voice in times of trouble. A personal thank you to Pat Lunny, Enniskillen, for taking the pictures.

All profits from *A Little Bit of Healing* will be donated to charity.

PART ONE

People who help me heal

Archbishop Denis Hurley

There are people who influence our lives more than we imagine. 35 years ago when I was working in the Communications Centre in Booterstown, a tall dignified cleric visited us. He wanted to see what we did and wondered if something similar could be set up in his own archdiocese.

I was impressed by his interest in communications, his Irish roots, interest in hurling and, most of all, his foresight in wanting to have the best for his archdiocese.

He was the then Archbishop of Durban in South Africa whose ancestors came from Ireland. After that I kept a keen eye on the life and times of Archbishop Denis Hurley.

Apartheid was a scourge in South Africa in the 1970s and he was the most powerful anti-apartheid voice in South Africa at the time, apart from Nelson Mandela. Yet in the midst of all the chaos he was planning to have the best possible facilities for his people and priests. That's optimism.

I met him a few times after that and discovered his reputation in South Africa was second to none. For many, Archbishop Desmond Tutu is rightly regarded as the voice of the oppressed. But the initial Christian condemnation of apartheid, heroically, came from Denis Hurley.

There is a book on his life called *Guardian of the Light: Archbishop Denis Hurley: Renewing the Church, Opposing Apartheid.* I have been reading extracts from it and I look forward to reading it in full.

Denis Hurley had a fascinating life within the church.

As far back as 1951 he was made a bishop at the age of 31 and was then the youngest bishop in the entire Catholic Church. He began drafting a series of pastoral letters denouncing apartheid 'as a blasphemy' and 'intrinsically evil'. He took on the might of an oppressive government. He organised, and marched in, demonstrations alongside Archbishop Tutu and Alan Paton. He encouraged Catholic schools in his diocese to start admitting non white students. He opposed the security forces and found himself charged with sedition. He eventually won the case and got 25,000

Rand from the South African government for malicious prosecution.

He began his journey to the priesthood at the age of 16 and he received part of his training here in Ireland. The most influential part of his preparation was the seven years he spent as a student in Rome. He made a deep impression on the Roman Church and when he went back to be a curate in the cathedral in Durban he used his European eyes to see the evil of ethnic separation. Unfortunately for him, his own white congregation didn't want to hear his condemnation of apartheid.

However, Rome made him a bishop at the age of 31 and a short time afterwards he became the Archbishop of Durban.

He was then enthused by the Second Vatican Council. He learned a whole new theology from the greatest theologians in the world and got to know radical bishops like Helder Camara of Recife in Brazil. He was convinced the way ahead for the church was to encourage Catholics everywhere to seek justice for the poor.

After the Council, Hurley joined with Nelson Mandela and others in the long fight for racial justice.

It was at this point that Hurley ran foul of Roman authority. Pope Paul VI brought out *Humanae Vitae* but Hurley told his people that the Pope, 'should not be laying down laws for the community without a good knowledge of the needs and conditions of the community'.

The Pope wrote directly to him and there was a terse exchange between the two men. Later still Archbishop Hurley wrote for the influential magazine *Theological Studies*. The subject he was asked to discuss was population control and the Catholic conscience.

In it he said the church should be more interested in changing the social structures which keep people poor and oppressed than imposing impossible burdens on them. The authorities tried to block the publication of the article but failed. Effectively it meant that Archbishop Hurley was regarded with suspicion in Rome and never became a Cardinal even though he was the most obvious choice.

At the end of his life in 2002 he attended the ordination of two women in the Anglican Church and addressed the congregation. He told the congregation, 'Don't tell the Pope … but when I get to heaven I shall do my best to promote the idea of women's ordination.'

Hurley is one of the unsung heroes of the Christian churches in Africa. He served his diocese in Durban for 41 years. He is regarded by many as 'the best Cardinal Africa never had'.

I am delighted that the man who impressed me so much, 35 years ago, always remained a real hero: men like him are sadly lacking in our church today.

St Brigid

Officially the season of spring this year begins on 20 March. That's when night and day will be about nearly the same length. It's called the spring equinox.

But in Celtic culture the first of February was the first day of spring. Those people who lived by their senses, recognised nature rolling over and waking from its winter slumber. They welcomed hardy flowers peeking above the earth: back then they also talked about a 'stretch in the evenings' in early February.

The first day of spring is one thing; the first spring day is quite another. So we know that Mother Nature can snap back to nasty winter weather at any time: but that all-consuming darkness is over and we look forward with hope to brighter days and brighter times.

One of the great saints of spring in Celtic spirituality is Saint Brigid, patroness of Ireland whose feast is celebrated on 1 February. She lived at the end of the fifth century, which makes much of her life-story uncertain. But I love the legends. She was a feisty lady, whose name means 'fiery arrow' and who held her own in a man's world. She took on bishops and beat them. As the Abbess of Kildare, she did things her way. She organised one of the first convents in history and gave women a real voice in the church.

It's said that she was a slave when she was first attracted to the Christian way of life. But then she gave so much of her owner's goods away to the poor that it was cheaper to grant her freedom. She even gave a valuable sword to a poor man so that he could sell it for food, thereby turning an instrument of war into something live-giving. We could learn from her. Use the money wasted on war and killing to keep the hungry alive.

Legend says that she often turned water into milk and then churned the milk to make butter. She gave the butter to the needy. Butter was meant for the rich only. At a different level, she once turned water into beer to satisfy the thirst of priests who visited her convent. And in one of the stories associated with her, it's said that she gave a visiting bishop so much beer that he made Brigid a bishop before he left. So you can see that the issue of women priests and women bishops is not as modern as we might think.

And here's a quotation from Brigid's life which I can safely say you won't find in any other saintly handbook. She said:

I would like a great lake of beer for the King of Kings
I would like the people of heaven
to be drinking it through time eternal.

What a great saint to herald the first day of spring! Both heaven and spring are getting more attractive by the second.

Mother Teresa of Calcutta

Blessed Teresa, or more famously, Mother Teresa of Calcutta, was born on 26 August 1910. She was baptised on 27 August 1910 and always celebrated the 27th as her birthday. Even non-believers know who Mother Teresa was. Her name is synonymous with doing good. You can either agree or disagree with her, but you can't argue with the good she did.

The novelist John McGahern had his own searching to do and for much of his life had a worthy battle with the institutional church. His father, it appears, was a pious man more than a religious man. He went strictly by the rule book. Being a sergeant, he believed that if you kept the law, you'd be safe.

On the other hand his mother, to whom McGahern was close, was a school teacher and was more gentle, more spiritual and more real. As he says himself, 'Catholicism cast a long shadow over all aspects of Irish society in the 1950s.'

In an interview with John Scally, McGahern's father has an insightful piece about parish missions given by the Redemptorists: 'They only make the pious a bit more insufferable and the sinner a bit more despairing ... trying to get people to change their life by ranting and raving is about as sensible as trying to cut turf with a razor blade.'

However, when it came to Mother Teresa, McGahern wrote: 'Mother Teresa's great value for Catholics and non-believers alike was to remind us that religion can and should be a thing of beauty. Illuminated by inexhaustible reserves of mercy and mission – a faith that inspires ... she showed us that the primary obligation is not to build memorials to the dead but to give food to the living.'

That's a sizable legacy for anyone to leave.

The woman who left that legacy was brought up in the old Yugoslavia. Her baptismal name was Agnes. Her mother Drana was her inspiration. As the family gathered to eat, her mother always reminded them: 'Never eat a single mouthful unless you share something with others.'

When Agnes was a teenager she decided to join the Loreto nuns. She came to Ireland for some of her formation and was now called Sr Teresa. She went to India to teach geometry in a Loreto School. At that time she wrote a letter to her mother telling her about the fine school it was, the beautiful children and how bright and well dressed and well fed they were. Her mother wrote a letter which became significant. In it she reminded Teresa, 'Don't forget you went to India to help the poor.' Then she reminded her of how they used to take people in who had nobody to help them in their family home. She recalled one woman they had cared for whose 'biggest hurt was loneliness'.

That had an impact on Teresa. On 10 December 1946 at the age of 37 she was on a train heading to Darjeeling for a personal retreat. She says that on the train she heard a call from God. It was 'a call within a call to care for the poorest of the poor'. Eventually she got permission to leave the Loreto convent to work in the slums with the poor. There were no facilities there. She taught the children the alphabet by tracing the letters with a stick in the dust.

One day while Teresa was living in this poor area, she met a woman who was extremely ill. She took her to the hospital in Calcutta. The hospital said she was an old dying woman and therefore they could do nothing for her. They told Teresa to take her away from the hospital because the hospital had enough to do caring for the sick who might live.

Teresa, remembering what her mother had told her, took the old woman in and looked after her until she died. Soon word got around and from that small one single act grew the Missionaries of Charity. Other people looked for help, more people came to help. Mother Teresa once said, 'I am a little pencil in the hand of God.'

The Missionaries of Charity were founded in 1950. Mother Teresa, in the meantime, in 1979 won a Nobel Peace Award for her work with the poor, yet when she died in 1997, there were 4500 nuns in her Order working in 133 countries.

She said the secret was to work for God. An American crew came to do a documentary. They followed her around as she washed the maggots out of the leprous wounds of the dying people on the streets. Her young nuns helped her throughout the day. The American said to her, 'Mother Teresa, I wouldn't do what you did for a million dollars a day.' Mother Teresa replied, 'Neither would I, but I do it for the love of God. Every person is Christ for me. The person I'm meeting is the only person in the world.'

There were those who objected to the work she did. There were 15 million people in Calcutta, 2 million of them were in poverty. 200,000 of them lived in the streets. People said she was a mere sticking plaster, doing little good. Her caring was a drop in the ocean and allowed the authorities off the hook. She should be working to change society rather than just helping in an insignificant way. Her answer was, 'God has not called me to be successful; God called me to be faithful.' To others she said, 'Our *work* is to help the poor; our *vocation* is to love God.'

During the many times I met her, she constantly emphasised that everyone has to find their own Calcutta. Not everyone is called to do the work she did, but each of us is called to do something. We should ask ourselves each morning, 'Is there one person I can help this day?' She gave the example of a dying child who was brought into her home by a policeman. Mother Teresa told one of her nuns: 'Hold that little baby until she dies. Love her into heaven.'

One of the great lessons from Mother Teresa's life is that we don't have to be perfect. During the last interview I did with her at Knock, she made it quite clear to me that there were times when she did not feel close to God. She even found it hard to believe that God approved what she was doing.

There were times when she had no peace of mind and was not sure that what she was doing was the work of God.

It seemed unbelievable at that time. Yet years later, her confessor wrote a book as part of the process for canonisation and in it he revealed that for 50 years Mother Teresa struggled with faith. He said she was overcome by doubts. She doubted her own goodness. She admitted, 'Nothing touches my soul.' But she kept on doing good. 'If you do good you'll be hurt,' she told me, 'but keep on doing good.'

In trying, confusing and difficult times, just keep on doing what you know to be right and, even though you can't believe in God, God will reveal God's goodness in God's good time. I'll leave you with her special prayer. It was composed by Mother Teresa as a rule of life for her and for us.

People are often unreasonable, irrational, and self-centred. Forgive them anyway.

If you are kind, people may accuse you of selfish, ulterior motives. Be kind anyway.

If you are successful, you will win some unfaithful friends and some genuine enemies. Succeed anyway.

If you are honest and sincere people may deceive you. Be honest and sincere anyway.

What you spend years creating, others could destroy overnight. Create anyway.

If you find serenity and happiness, some may be jealous. Be happy anyway.

The good you do today, will often he forgotten. Do good anyway.

Give the best you have, and it will never be enough. Give your best anyway.

In the final analysis, it is between you and God.

It was never between you and them anyway.

Jean Donovan

Jean Donovan is one of my heroes. She was born into an upper middle-class family in Connecticut – that's important when you see what she did.

When she was in college she came to Ireland to find out about her ancestors. During that visit she met a priest who worked with the poor in South America. He explained how the American government was actually oppressing the poor. He challenged her to do something with her life to help the poor.

She went back to college and graduated with distinction before taking a senior post in accountancy. She progressed up the ranks but then suddenly, in 1977, she quit to become a lay missionary in El Salvador.

She got to know at first hand the brutality which the corrupt regime in El Salvador carried out with the support of the American government. She had to help the nuns bury children, killed by government agencies, whose bodies had been left at the side of the road.

Donovan was inspired by the sermons of Archbishop Oscar Romero. On the 24 March 1980, Romero who had done so much to help the poor, was shot dead as he was celebrating Mass.

Just after Romero's death, two of her friends were brutally murdered as they walked her home.

This had a traumatic effect on her and she left El Salvador, first of all to visit her family in Miami, then to visit her boyfriend in London and finally to come back to Ireland where she once again met the priest who had asked her to do something with her life. She realised now that she would find it impossible to go back to El Salvador. But on her way back home she again went into a church in Miami near her parents' house and when she came out, those who saw her knew instantly that she had changed. She discerned that she now must answer the call of the poor and help them in their search for justice.

A few weeks later, on 2 December 1980, Jean Donovan and Dorothy Kazel went to meet their friends and co-workers, two

Maryknoll nuns, Ita Forde and Maura Clarke at the airport. None of the four was seen alive again.

A few days later the bodies of all four were found in a shallow grave near the roadside on the way home from the airport. All four were beaten and then shot in the head from close range. Jean Donovan was also raped, and was so badly beaten that she was unrecognisable. She died at the age of 27.

To add insult to injury, the US Secretary of State said: 'The nuns were not just nuns, the nuns were also political activists on behalf of the guerrillas.' He accused the nuns of running a road-block. All of which was obviously untrue.

The fact of the matter is that the three nuns and Jean Donovan, in their own different ways, were making the poor their first option in life, believing that the effective witness to the gospel is inseparable from solidarity with the oppressed.

Sr Ita Forde had written to her 16 year old niece: 'This is a terrible time for the youth of El Salvador. A lot of idealism is snuffed out here. Yet … people here have found a meaning to live, to sacrifice, struggle and even die. And whether their life spans sixteen years or sixty, for them their life has had a purpose. In many ways they are fortunate people … I hope you can come to find that which gives a deep meaning for you. Somebody that enthuses you and enables you to keep moving ahead.'

The four women died not just for their faith but for the poor. That had previously been put in context by Oscar Romero shortly before his death when he said: 'One who has committed to the poor must risk the same fate as the poor. And in El Salvador we know what the fate of the poor signifies – to disappear, to be tortured, to be captured and to be found dead.'

Ghandi

Ghandi often said that from a theoretical point of view he was impressed by the principles of Christianity. He said he could never become a Christian 'because he never met anybody who put those principles into action'.

When he was working in South Africa, he tried to help the people of mixed race there. He was unsuccessful and had to leave the country to go back to India. But whilst he was still in Africa he found himself rushing for a train. It was overcrowded. Poor people were packed into the carriages. In the rush one of his sandals slipped off.

When he got on the train he looked out the window and saw a number of people fighting over his sandal. He lowered the window and threw out his other sandal. He reasoned that he was never going to get his sandal back and that one sandal was no good to either of them. So he threw his other sandal into the crowd so that the finder at least would have two sandals. That's a practical way of putting Christ's care for others into action.

Here are seven situations which Ghandi regarded as utterly dangerous. These he prioritised as:

1) Politics without principle.
2) Wealth without work.
3) Business without morality.
4) Pleasure without conscience.
5) Education without direction.
6) Science without compassion.
7) Prayer without sacrifice.

We could do worse than apply those seven deadly sins to our own lives to make sure we're not guilty. That's why we pray the Our Father. 'Thy Kingdom come, thy will be done on earth.' That's the Kingdom of God in action.

Martin Buber

I love people's personal stories, particularly those who are not perfect. I was reading a story from the life of Martin Buber, the Jewish philosopher, recently which impressed me. At the beginning of the 20th century he wrote one of his most powerful books called *I And Thou*. Very briefly he said there are two basic ways of treating the people we meet: the I/It meeting or the I/Thou meeting.

In the I/It encounter we treat the other person as an object to be used and cast aside when it suits us. Sometimes we even treat ourselves in the same disrespectful manner. More frequently it's how we treat God. God is dragged into our life only when we need him and is often completely forgotten when he has served our purposes.

On the other hand the I/Thou relationship is much deeper. It happens when two genuine, good persons really meet. We see a person with real human feelings, with dreams, with needs and we treat that other person with dignity and respect. In the process, according to Buber, the other person receives affirmation from meeting us and we get life from them.

Buber went on to explain why he wrote *I and Thou*. During the First World War he was fully engaged writing another book of philosophy. He spent all his waking hours thinking and writing. One day a young man came seeking his advice. He had been conscripted into the German army to fight in the First World War. But the young man was in a dilemma. If he went to war, even though he was a pacifist, he knew that if he were killed, he'd waste the many gifts God gave him. Furthermore in war he would have to kill others and snuff out their gifts long before their time. On the other hand, if he refused to go to war somebody would be sent in his place and that would be their life wasted. That was his dilemma and that's why he came to Buber.

Buber was pre-occupied with his own writing at the time and gave him a brief hearing. He said, 'It's your life, think about it seriously, do what you think is right, and that will be right.' The man went off disillusioned. Sadly, that evening he took his own life. Buber admits he never got over that. He knew he had treated the man as an object. He dismissed him as interruption. He didn't treat him as a human being with a real dilemma. He wrote the book *I And Thou*, to make up for his mistake.

Which goes to prove what I've always believed – our mistakes can destroy us; but they can also make us, if we have enough humility and courage to learn from them.

St Francis

When it comes to saints, there is none more popular than St Francis. He's loved by everybody, even those who don't have much interest in religion. It was 800 years ago, in 1209, that he gathered his first Franciscan companions around him. Today there are 650,000 people worldwide who practise Franciscan spirituality.

I've always loved his radical spirit, his simplicity, his love of nature and of animals. I am inspired by his respect for creation and the earth. On his deathbed he asked to be placed, lying naked, on the clay floor so that he could die like Jesus did.

Being naked became something of a habit with Francis. When he decided to leave the good life behind him and heard the voice of God asking him 'to repair the church which is in ruins,' he took it literally. He sold some of his father's property and began repairing his local run down church. His father brought him before the bishop to get him to repent. Francis impetuously stripped off his clothes and, standing naked before them, said: 'I used to call you father but from now on I have only one Father – our father who art in heaven.'

He believed that our whole way of life should be a sermon. 'We should preach the gospel at all times and when necessary we may even use words,' he told his followers.

Francis left us few writings. One of our best loved prayers now is always referred to as the prayer of St Francis. 'Lord, make me an instrument of your peace' is so typically Francis that most people are convinced that he actually wrote it.

I'm sorry to disillusion you. Nobody knows for certain who wrote it, but it was probably a French priest around 1912, 700 years after Francis. It was during the Second World War that this prayer for peace began circulating as the Prayer of St Francis:

Lord make me an instrument of your peace,
where there is hatred, let me sow love.
Where there is injury, let me sow pardon.
Where there is doubt, let me sow faith.
Where there is despair, let me sow hope.

Where there is darkness, let me give light.
Where there is sadness, let me give joy.

St Francis did not write these powerful words, but what's important is that he lived them.

So should we.

Elvis Presley

Elvis Presley died in 1977. The fact that his music is still selling in millions, shows the enormous star Elvis was.

I admit I was and still am a dedicated Elvis fan. There's something about his music that touches me. Put on a Presley track and I'm totally hooked, especially his early, raw recordings. In the fifties, Elvis Presley invented pop culture. John Lennon said: 'Before Elvis there was nothing.' Bruce Springsteen agreed: 'It was like he came along and whispered a dream in everybody's ear, and then we dreamt it.'

The other icon of the time was Pat Boone who, unlike Presley, was the son every mother wanted. Boone and Presley vied for Number One in the charts, but were close friends in real life. When I talked with Pat Boone he told me that Presley was a shy, modest and good mannered man who often acted as a baby-sitter for the Boones. That's the human side of the superstar.

Presley is often remembered for the sad way he died. That's what disturbed me when I visited his home, Gracelands, in Memphis Tennessee some years ago. I was on my own, moving from room to room in a house that has remained unchanged since his death. It was weird to pick over the relics of a hero's home. There was a room where the carpet covered the floors, continued up the walls and across the ceiling. There was a kitchen where Elvis hung out with friends.

There was the trophy room with close on 250 Gold discs fixed to the walls. That's success. There was the burial grounds where he, his mother Gladys, twin brother Jesse and father Vernon have tombs. He left 8 cars, 6 motorbikes, 2 aeroplanes, 16 televisions, and 5 bank accounts with $2million in each of them.

Yet at 3:30 am on 16 August 1977 he was found dead on the bathroom floor, suffering from heart failure at 42 years of age. He was lonely, depressed, bloated and abusing drugs.

What got to me was that this man who brought such freedom, such glamour, such joy, such excitement to me and to countless millions, was himself a prisoner of fame, trapped by the demands of fans and management.

I often wonder what he would be like now in his late seventies. Is there a part of me which is secretly glad he died young so that we don't have to face the passing of youth ourselves? Life, fame and fortune pass for all of us eventually. We'd better have something worthwhile to base our eternity on.

John Henry Newman

When Pope Benedict came to Britain, he celebrated the life and times of an extraordinary man known as John Henry Newman. Newman is probably best remembered for writing the hymn 'Lead Kindly Light'.

Before that his constant search to find a home within Christianity is, for me, hugely encouraging. Newman was born in 1801, was ordained as an Anglican priest and went on to found the Oxford Movement. In 1845 he became a Roman Catholic. As you might expect, he was viewed with suspicion both by Anglicans and Roman Catholics. That's what happens to people when they bravely follow God's spirit. Towards the end of his life he was made a Cardinal and died at the age of 89. His writings became his greatest legacy to society, to religion and education. It is generally accepted now that he helped to inspire the Second Vatican Council in the 1960s. He once wrote: 'To live is to change and to have changed often is to be perfect,' and he certainly lived that challenge in his own life.

He was regarded as a saintly man. And eight years ago when an American Deacon named Jack Sullivan recovered from a serious spinal disorder, doctors and theologians in Rome came to the conclusion that Sullivan was cured as a result of Newman's intersession. Pope Benedict declared the healing to be a miracle. This means that Cardinal Newman is now known as Blessed in recognition of his extraordinary virtue. He could be declared a saint later.

Newman's journey in faith from darkness to light is beautifully summed up in his most lasting work:

'Lead, kindly light, amid the encircling gloom,
Lead thou me on.'

A perfect thought for any day.

Helder Camara

Just over one hundred years ago, one of the most significant Christian men of the last century was born. Dom Helder Camara was the Archbishop of Recife when he died in 1999. By then he was revered and held as a saint by his people.

He was born in Brazil, the twelfth of thirteen children. By the age of 8 he had his mind made up to become a priest. But his father, who was far from religious, said to him, 'Do you know what it means to be a priest? It means to belong to yourself no more. The priest belongs to God and to others.' To which young Helder replied, 'That is exactly what I want to be.'

In his early priesthood he was right wing and conservative. But within a few years he became the leader of Radical Non Violent Movement for Justice. In the 1930s he was transferred to Rio De Janeiro where he became an auxiliary bishop in 1952. He organised social services for the poor, but came to the conclusion that charity was not enough. What we needed was justice. That in turn meant empowering people to be able to change their own lives.

In 1964 he was made Archbishop of Recife which coincided with a brutal military coup. Camara immediately became the spokesman for those who opposed the oppressive regime, for which he earned the title 'The Red Bishop'.

But he led by example. Instead of having all the trimmings of a bishop, he dressed in a simple cream soutane with a small wooden cross instead of the golden pectoral cross.

He moved out of the bishop's palace and lived in small rooms beside the sacristy. He encouraged lay people to be trained and was the first to open seminary doors to lay people and women. It was said that his door was always open to anyone in genuine need. Among those who knocked at his door was a hired assassin. When Dom Helder answered the door and identified himself, the gunman was so undone by sight of this frail bishop that he abandoned his mission. 'I can't kill you,' he said, 'You are one of the Lord's.'

It was only one of many attacks which Dom Helder survived.

For 13 years he was banned by the military government from any public speaking whatsoever. The newspapers were not even permitted to mention his name. Although he himself survived, his biggest pain was to see that many of his colleagues, priests, catechists and lay people were imprisoned, tortured and killed simply because of their friendship with him.

He said the source of this strength came from his prayer. He got up every night at 2 o'clock and prayed till 4. His day began again at 6am.

But perhaps the greatest pain suffered by Dom Helder Camara came from within his own church. When he retired as Archbishop of Recife, the conservative successor reversed almost every single one of his initiatives to help the poor. He had to suffer the pain of seeing his lifetime's work disappear.

In one of his most telling quotes he said: 'When I feed the poor I am called a saint. But if I ask why the poor have no food I am called a communist.'

The Vatican has been asked to begin the process of canonisation, but so far there has been little response.

Viktor Frankl

In *Man's Search For Meaning*, Dr Viktor Frankl writes of the unspeakable horrors he witnessed as a prisoner in Nazi death camps during World War II. The book is not just a record of atrocities, but a testament of what he learned about the meaning of life from his experiences and from his fellow prisoners.

When he was arrested, Frankl tried to hide a book he had been writing on psychiatry inside his coat. The manuscript was his life's work. But at Auschwitz all his possessions and clothes – including his coat – were taken from him, and his manuscript was lost forever.

Frankl writes: 'I had to surrender my clothes and in turn inherited the worn-out rags of an inmate who had been sent to the gas chamber immediately after his arrival at the Auschwitz railway station. Instead of the many pages of my manuscript, I found in the pocket of my newly acquired coat one single page torn out of a Hebrew prayer book, containing the most important Jewish prayer: "The Lord our God is Lord alone! Therefore you shall love the Lord your God with all your heart".'

Frankl interpreted the 'coincidence' as a challenge to suffer bravely. 'Life has a meaning up to the last moment, and it retains this meaning literally to the end,' he wrote.

When he survived, Frankl went ahead and wrote a book which was quite different from the one he lost with his coat. It became a life-changing book for himself and for those who read it. He was convinced that he couldn't have written this book if he hadn't experienced loss and taken on board what he learned. He couldn't have written *Man's Search For Meaning* if the manuscript had not been lost and if he had not been changed by the prayer he found in the rags of the old man who was ready to face death.

Life teaches us wisdom if we are wise enough to listen.

Jean Vanier

Since Mother Teresa died, Jean Vanier is everyone's idea of what a living saint should be. He has devoted his entire life to caring for, and learning from, the broken and the handicapped. Yet when I have spoken to him he has made me feel uncomfortable. His holiness, his dedication, challenge me to look at the futility of my own life. Mother Teresa had exactly the same effect on me.

Vanier was born in Geneva in 1928. He's the son of a former Governor General of Canada, George Vanier and his wife Pauline.

His father was an Ambassador to France during the Second World War, where Jean Vanier saw inmates arriving from concentration camps who looked like skeletons. That vision marked him for life. The evil which human beings perpetrate on other human beings led him to study philosophy in an effort to find an answer. Even though he was successful, his life demanded something more.

Vanier was also an Officer in the Royal Navy and in the Canadian Navy. So in 1950 he resigned and joined a small community of students, mostly lay, to work with the poor in France. Their aim was to foster prayer and study. At one point in his life he wanted to be a priest but thankfully he recognised his particular calling as a layman.

Eventually he bought a small dilapidated house called L'Arche, (which means the Ark – Noah's Ark). There he welcomed two mentally handicapped men to share his home with him. It was the beginning of the hugely successful L'Arche communities.

It is a system which pairs a person who has special needs with a person who hasn't. The aim is to encourage people rejected by society and to give them their proper place. They believe everyone is unique and sacred with a right to friendship, communion and a spiritual life. He says L'Arche is not out to change the world but 'to create little places where love is possible'.

Vanier Communities received international attention in the mid-eighties when Fr Henri Nouwen, a Catholic priest whose spiritual books sold millions, settled in a L'Arche community in

Canada. Nouwen had been searching for peace all his life without success. He was an academic, a major writer, commentator on the church in South America. But it was in L'Arche that he found his home before his untimely death.

There are now 104 L'Arche Communities in 30 countries on five continents.

Vanier has the brain of a philosopher and the heart of a saint. He frequently talks about one of the original members of L'Arche who taught him the value of touch:

> He does not understand much, but he does understand whether we touch him with love. Our bodies are called to be instruments of grace. We must learn to touch with tenderness. Touch has become sexualised in our culture, but it is so vitally important to reveal to people their value and give them security.

John Moriarty

Good Stories shorten the road and this is a very good story indeed.

The philosopher and mystic, the late John Moriarity, told a beautiful story about his life and struggles after he came back from Canada where he lectured in philosophy.

He became almost a recluse in Connemara to empty his brain of all the learned knowledge which cluttered up his mind.

After a while he had to pay some bills, so he got a job working in an ancient castle in the West. He washed dishes. There was a part of the hotel where young waitresses used to come in to the kitchen with their dirty dishes and because the lino was worn they often slipped. The owner of the hotel decided to put down very expensive non-slip lino on that floor.

A local handyman was called upon. He was a handyman in name only. Much of his work was not of the highest quality, technically.

John watched him from a height, cutting this very expensive lino to put down around the uneven walls of the castle kitchen. He was making a complete botch of it, cutting it with a crude knife in a zig zag fashion.

John cautiously said to him, 'Perhaps I haven't the straightest eye in the world, but I don't think that's the best way to cut it.'

The old man was on his knees, knife in hand, slashing the lino. He looked over his shoulder and waited half a minute before speaking. When he did speak he didn't say it angrily. And what he said was:

'John, this is a lovely old place and in a lovely old place like this, the only good way to cut anything straight is to cut it crooked.'

And John, being a philosopher went home that night and thought about it. He walked up along the hilly, crooked roads and he noticed that if they were straight roads nobody would ever use them. They'd be too steep.

And he saw the rivers, crooked and meandering. And the

water was purified by the very crookedness of the bank. And the life that was in them was because they were crooked. And the beauty that was in them was because they were crooked. Canals on the other hand are 'dead straight'.

And then his mind went back to a night in his youth. He remembered an old man who was fond of a drink. Some days when he'd wake up and see the vast expanse of Irish countryside in front of him, his head couldn't take it in.

And since he had no Shrink to go to, he often went to the pub instead. John said that in America they go to Shrinks; the world is too big, the vision inside the head is too big to comprehend so they go to people to shrink their vision so that they can cope. But this old man had no Shrink, Arthur Guinness was a better companion. Or so he thought.

One Christmas Eve, he was in the pub. Just before Midnight Mass he was put out so that they could close the pub in time for Mass. As he left he bought three huge bottles of stout and dropped them into his overcoat pockets with a gentle clinking sound. Then he went to Mass and stayed at the back of the church.

The Offertory Procession came and two young girls, at home from a convent boarding school, brought up the gifts. They did it perfectly. Their hair was combed and shinny. They were dressed in spotless clothes.

They walked in unison in a straight line as they brought the gifts up. And they bowed together and they didn't crash into each other, and they turned and walked down and they genuflected as straight as rods and their mother was proud of them.

The congregation bowed their heads to welcome Jesus at the consecration at midnight Mass. Just then some became aware of a rustle in the body of the church. The old man with his big black coat and his Wellington boots began to stagger in crooked lines up the chapel. And everybody wanted to grab him but nobody did because they were afraid and they respected him.

He reached the altar rails and opened the gate because he was used to opening gates to let cattle through. He closed the gates behind him because you always close gates in the country.

He made his meandering way to the altar and the priest looked at him gently and the old man said 'Good evening, Father.' And the priest said, 'Good evening.'

And he reached down into his big black coat pocket and he took out a bottle of stout and he left it on the altar. He said, 'Excuse me, Father, but I just wanted to stand Jesus a drink for Christmas.'

And then he stumbled back through the gate and staggered his way in crooked lines down the aisle. It was at that point that the congregation realised that there's no need to be straight; for God can write straight on crooked lines. There is no need to be perfect and a heart which is sincere is always beautiful no matter what the body looks like.

The road to Calvary was twisted and crooked. And Jesus' body was twisted and broken when it was taken down from the Cross. And Mary's heart was twisted in grief.

Maybe there's a lot to be said about a life that's lost and meandering yet genuinely seeking God. Maybe it's right to go down the side roads *he* leads me.

In John Moriarity's story, he returned to the old castle the morning after he noticed the crooked rivers and paths and went to see how the handyman's botched lino looked. He discovered that it fitted perfectly into every nook and corner of the castle's crooked floors and walls.

The philosopher then knew for certain that the handyman was absolutely right when he said: 'John, remember this is a lovely old castle, in a lovely old place, and in a lovely old place like this, the only good way to cut anything straight is to cut it crooked.'

Nelson Mandela

Nelson Mandela is the most significant political leader of the past 50 years.

One of the most frequently quoted sayings of Nelson Mandela comes from his inauguration speech in 1994. The quotation is often attributed to him, but he borrowed it from another source. It embodies the philosophy of this magnanimous man:

> Our deepest fear is not that we are inadequate. Our deepest fear is that we are powerful beyond measure.
>
> It is our light, not our darkness that most frightens us.
>
> We ask ourselves who am I to be brilliant ...? Actually who are you not to be? You are a child of God. Your playing small does not serve the world. There is nothing enlightened about shrinking so that other people won't feel insecure around you.
>
> You are born to shine and manifest the glory of God that is within you. It is not just some of us. It is everyone. And as we let our light shine, we unconsciously give other people permission to do the same. As we're liberated from our own fear, our presence automatically liberates others.

Nelson Mandela continues to give hope to the downtrodden. In his book, *Long Walk To Freedom,* he reports vividly on what it was like for a black person to grow up in the evil system of apartheid.

As a young man he lived in Alexandra – a township in Johannesburg which still exists today. He admits that life in Alexandra was both exciting and frightening. It was a poor place and dangerous too. It was called the dark city for many reasons, one of which was that it had no electricity.

'But Alex was also a special place,' writes Mandela.'It was one of the few places where Africans could own property and, more or less, run their own affairs ... I lived in a shack at the back of a house. It had a dirt floor, no heating, no electricity and no running water. But it was a place of my own and I was happy to have it.

'Like most other people in Alex I was poor. The law firm that I worked for paid me a salary of two pounds per week. Most of this money went towards paying my rent. I still had to find money for food, transport, university fees and most important of all, candles. I needed candles to study at night because I could not afford a paraffin lamp.'

To save money he walked six miles morning and evening to and from work.

'I often went for days without more than a mouthful of food and without a change of clothing. Mr Sidelsky (his employer) was my height – once gave me an old suit. I wore that same suit every day for five years. In the end there were more patches than suit.'

In time he became leader of the African National Congress. As a lawyer he was one of the chief organisers and leading strategists in their fight against white oppression. On many occasions he was taken to court and eventually in 1964 was sentenced to life imprisonment on Roben Island. That was a miracle, because most thought he would receive the death penalty.

In his book he tells what it was like in prison. He and four others were chained together and put in a police van that had no windows to be transported to the prison. 'We drove all night and arrived at Cape Town docks the following afternoon. Still chained, we were put onto an old wooden ferry and taken downstairs. The only light and air came from a small window above. This window had another use: the warders enjoyed urinating through it onto us.'

He concluded his famous speech from the dock: 'During my lifetime, I have dedicated myself to this struggle of the African people. I have fought against white domination and I have fought against black domination. I have cherished the idea of a democratically free society in which all persons live together in harmony and with equal opportunities. It is an ideal which I hope to live for and to achieve. But if needs be, it's an ideal for which I am prepared to die.'

Mandela was 46 years old when he was sent to Roben Island prison. The prisoners worked in a limestone quarry crushing stones with hammers. Watches and clocks were banned on the island.

'The night watch warder woke us up at 5.30 every morning by ringing a bell. After cleaning our cells and rolling up our mats and blankets we were let out to empty our toilet buckets. We ate break-fast in our cells during those first few months. We helped our-selves to porridge from an old metal drum and drank what was a poor excuse for coffee – ground up maze baked until it was black. … If the three buttons of our khaki jackets were undone, or if we did not lift our hats as the warders walked past or if our cells were untidy, they punished us with solitary confinement or with the loss of meals … We got our last meal of the day at 4.30 in the after-noon. It was mealie – pap with a carrot or a piece of cabbage or a beetroot thrown in. Every second day we got a small piece of meat with our porridge. The meat was usually gristle.'

As a D Group prisoner – the worst possible kind – Mandela was allowed to have one visitor and receive one letter every six months. He admits this was the heaviest burden of all.

When he was sentenced he became a 'non-person.' That meant nobody could speak about him, write about him, or talk about him or act on his behalf. He had no rights of any kind.

I was lucky enough to meet him in South Africa in a Radio stu-dio shortly after he was inaugurated as President. In a stroke of good fortune I was doing an interview about the album, 'Give Up Yer Aul Sins' on the national broadcasting station of South Africa, where I was working at the time. When I went into the building to await my interview the person on air was Nelson Mandela. He came out to the waiting room and I was introduced to him. I asked him if I could have a few moments of his time to do a quick inter-view for the *Sunday World*. He readily agreed and although the in-terview was brief it was one of the most memorable I have ever done.

One of the most difficult parts of being in jail, he told me, was that he lost contact with his family. When his mother died and when one of his children was killed in a car crash, he was not al-lowed to go to their funerals. He saw his then wife, Winnie Mandela for less than half an hour once every six months. This went on for 27 years until he was released.

However, over the 27 years he became great friends with one of the warders who treated him with dignity. He remained friends with him and invited his gaoler to his Inauguration Ceremony.

Typically he's a man who held very few grudges even though he had every right to.

I asked him if he was bitter about his treatment. It's an answer he has given often over the years and very effectively too. He says, 'If I held unto bitterness, I'd still be in prison.'

I also asked him to comment on the worldwide opinion of the time that he was a saint. He stopped and thought for a moment and then said, 'I'm not sure what a saint is. I am not a Christian. But somebody once told me that a saint is a sinner who tries harder. If that is the case then I am indeed a saint.'

He then went on to say that he wanted to be regarded as an ordinary human being with virtues and vices the same as every-body else.

He cast his first vote on 27 April 1994 at the age of 76. His was one of the millions of votes which put the ANC into power, making Nelson Mandela the first Black President of South Africa. The world has never been the same since.

The Simpsons

I'm a big fan of the Simpsons when I get a chance to see them. They've been the most dysfunctional family on television since 1987. Yet we often feel that if the Simpsons can survive, so can we. More than 60 million people watch them worldwide each week.

That figure got a boost recently when the official newspaper of the Vatican, *L'Osservatore Romano*, wrote favourably about the Simpsons. It was a shock for many traditionalists to see such a conservative paper encouraging the irreverent and often politically incorrect humour of Homer Simpson or the brashness of young Bart Simpson or the off-the-wall treatment of so many sacred cows. Bart once confessed: 'I've done many things I am not proud of, and those I am proud of are disgusting.'

Homer once mused about religion: 'What's that religion with all the well meaning rules that don't work out in real life? ... You know, Christianity.' Yet the Vatican paper suggested that without the 'tender and irreverent, scandalous and ironic, deranged and profound' programme, with its 'philosophical and at times even theological touches, today many would not know how to laugh'. To be fair, you'd find it hard to disagree with that.

L'Osservatore Romano went on to say that 'the relationship between God and man is one of the most important and most serious themes in the show. *The Simpsons* provides an intriguing mirror of the religious and spiritual confusion of our times,' they write. They mentioned, favourably, an episode where Homer climbs a heavenly staircase for a chat with God, who is seated behind a desk with a sign reading: 'I believe in me.'

Vatican approval comes after the Church of England began to use episodes of the Simpsons in Sunday school three years ago. I wonder had they heard Homer's thoughts on Sunday sermons. 'I'm not a bad guy,' he said, 'I work hard and I love my kids. So why should I spend half my Sunday hearing about how I'm going to hell?'

The Simpsons are now shown in Italy where some of the dialogue has to be changed to make it accessible. In America Mr Burns says: 'I'm as impotent as a Nevada Boxing Commissioner.' In Italy it's: 'as impotent as an old Christian Democrat.'

The Vatican quoted Pope Paul VI to justify its interest in all forms of communication. He said that nothing human is alien to the church, but I wonder how that applies to a cartoon family.

I'll leave you with another theological gem from Homer. When he was asked why he led such a blasphemous life, his reply was: 'Don't worry sweetheart, if I'm wrong I'll repent on my deathbed. Always have a back-up plan.' And that's good advice.

Richard Moore

One of the great stories to come out of Northern Ireland in recent years has been that of Richard Moore. As a young boy of ten years old he was blinded by a rubber bullet from a British solider in May 1972. That event has been well documented, as has Richard Moore's extraordinary ability to not only forgive the solider, but to dedicate his life to helping other children caught in war. *Children In Crossfire* is a world famous organisation which has the backing of even his Holiness the Dalai Lama.

The BBC made an incredible documentary about Richard which followed him in his search to find the solider who shot him. After initial suspicion between the two, they have now become friends. Forgiveness has been a key to that friendship.

In a fascinating book which he has written in conjunction with the author Don Mullan, Richard's story is brilliantly told. The title of the book, *Can I Give Him My Eyes?* is a phrase that Richard's late father used when he finally knew his son was blind and would never see again.

In the epilogue Richard tells us that the book is a story which covers those aspects of his life which he is willing to share. But it was his reflection on forgiveness which I found extraordinary. He says: 'One of the principle factors in helping me to cope with blindness was forgiveness. That I harboured no hatred towards the solider who shot me, or towards the British Army, freed me from the burden of bitterness. That I forgave the solider meant I wasn't carrying that baggage through my life. It left me free to deal with other things and with the practical issues around blindness, such as mobility and developing the necessary skills for the future. Acceptance was also very important in dealing with blindness. I learned very quickly that accepting I would never see again allowed me to focus on what I *could* do, rather than what I *couldn't*. I had to accept that I would never be able to drive a car or become a brain surgeon and you certainly wouldn't let me wire your house. All those things I had to accept were enough, without having to deal with anger, hatred and bitterness.'

There you get a flavour of the man. Common sense, humour and quite incredible insights. He goes on to talk about the foolishness of bitterness. 'When I thought about bitterness and anger, I could see they were self-destructive emotions that would affect no-one but me. Like a cancer, they would have destroyed me from the inside out, and I believe that I would not have been able to function as a full human being if I had been filled with such negative energy. Anything that I have achieved in life I believe I would not have achieved had I allowed anger and bitterness to be the dominant forces.'

Richard attributes this ability to forgive to his wonderful, faith-filled and loving parents. 'It was their total lack of bitterness. Furthermore, while they were more traumatised by my injuries than I was, they began to immediately focus on my future and all that I would need to cope. In truth I hadn't the time or luxury to be bitter or to become absorbed in self pity.'

Richard has met with his Holiness the Dalai Lama who writes the introduction to the book. In it he calls Richard Moore his hero.

Through Richard's own Christian upbringing and the influence of the Dalia Lama he realises: 'The process of forgiveness is not going to change the past. By forgiving the solider, I am not going to get my eyesight, but forgiveness can change the future, and that is what happened in my case.'

Richard is at pains to point out that if he can do it so can anyone. He used to say he was lucky that he was able to forgive but now he knows that luck had nothing to do with it. 'It was, quite simply, that I was blessed – blessed by the power of my parent's prayers. I genuinely believe it was the devotion of my mammy and my daddy and their prayers, that ultimately helped me to have such a positive and enjoyable life. Otherwise it is inexplicable.'

He mentions some of the advantages of being blind, even though he is at pains to point out that he never wants to make light of blindness or to belittle others who are blind. He talks about his utter dependency on others for many activities. Getting on a plane, finding a cup of tea at home or in a restaurant, signing a letter, cannot be done without the help of others and without others touching him. And Richard says: 'The simple act of guiding a person's hand to sign a letter or a document brings out compassion in the other. In a sense it's another gift of blindness.'

He explains clearly the slow process of how Charles, the soldier who blinded him, and he have grown in friendship.

Richard himself graduated from university, learned to play the guitar, is married to Rita, has two children, and as a family they have looked after the Folk Group in the Long Tower Chapel in Derry for years.

Yet he makes it quite clear that what happened shouldn't have happened: 'It would be remiss of me not to state that what happened to me was an injustice. My subsequent ability to cope doesn't take away from the fact that what happened to me was wrong. No child, no matter their colour, culture, background and location in the world should have to endure such trauma and suffering ...'

Can I Give Him My Eyes? is a moving, powerful description of a journey in darkness that has led inevitably to wonderful enlightenment. Richard concludes his epilogue: 'I've never forgotten the gem of wisdom my daddy gave me when I was a young teenager: "Never let one cloud spoil a sunny day." For me that cloud represented some aspects of blindness but I didn't allow it to spoil my sunny days of which, I am glad to say, there have been plenty.'

This is truly an inspiring story to help us through these dark times. (*Can I Give Him My Eyes?* by Richard Moore with Don Mullan is published by Hachette Books. www.hbgi.ie.)

Sojourner Truth

Michelle Obama unveiled a statue in Washington to honour one of her heroes, the amazing Sojouner Truth.

Sojourner Truth was born at the end of the 18th century and sold into slavery at the age of ten. She fought for the rights of women when it was dangerous.

She was owned by a Dutch slave-master in the state of New York. Like all slaves then, she had to take the name of the owner as her own.

She was one of 13 children, every one of whom in turn was sold into slavery. She had no say in the matter.

When her owner thought that as a slave she was nearing the end of her life, she was given her freedom. At once she changed her name. She said she always felt called by God to pursue truth and she now wanted to spend the rest of her life journeying around, helping, encouraging and, in some cases, cajoling people to seek freedom for slaves and civil rights for women. So she took the name Sojourner Truth. She lived to be over 80.

There are many stories about her. Once she was asked to preach in a Baptist church in the Deep South. A throng of admirers came to hear what she had to say. But the elders of the church felt uneasy when they met her. She was a large woman, over six feet tall. Her demeanour was masculine, her voice deep and resonant. Added to which, she smoked a foul-smelling, oversized pipe. Quietly the elders wondered if this was the real Sojourner. Was she someone out to trick them? Was she a woman at all? So they hit on a plan which they put to Sojourner as diplomatically as possible. They suggested that the lady's committee would meet her privately in a room and carry out their own discreet investigation. When they were satisfied that Sojourner was a woman, they would be delighted to hear her preach. But Sojourner was not to be doubted. There and then, she ripped open her blouse and in her best bass voice said: 'These breasts of mine have suckled many children of white people – children who should have been given milk by their own mothers when my own children were left hungry and crying. If you still doubt me, come and try them yourself.' Sojourner preached.

On another occasion, some of her friends were anxious about her smoking. They were not too happy about the smell from the pipe or, for that matter, the indignity of a famous woman smoking a pipe at all.

A friend said gently: 'Sojourner, you know that you are a venerable lady now. We hope you don't die for many years and we are sure you won't. Yet, you should be careful. All this pipe smoking is not good for you and if you don't stop smoking it could be that the Good Lord will be none too happy to let you into heaven with the awful breath you have from that stinking pipe.'

Sojourner took the pipe from her mouth and spat out: 'Friends, when I goes to the Good Lord, I sure as hell intend to leave my breath behind me here. I knows the Good Lord won't have to deal with that problem.'

She once came uninvited to a rally which was demanding equal voting rights for women in Ohio in 1852. Many of the more genteel were hoping she wouldn't come at all. They were astounded when she charged into the meeting.

As she arrived, there were many clergymen, as usual, arguing against the equality of women. One was explaining how the Lord chose twelve apostles and none of them was a woman. 'If the Lord wanted women to be equal he would have chosen some women amongst them. And of course it was of no small import that the Good Lord was, in any case, a man himself.'

Sojourner did not wait to be invited but gave a long speech outlining her own life and that of other women. She finished with the immortal reminder:

As you say, the Good Lord was indeed a man. But when the Good Lord came to be made man, it was arranged between God and woman. And man had nothing to do with it.

That's why Sojourner Truth is Michelle Obama's hero and why she's mine too.

Thomas Merton

I don't know if the name Thomas Merton means much to you. But he means a lot to me. He's been a hero of mine for more than 40 years ever since he died on 10 December 1968.

It's impossible to tell you why someone's spiritual journey can be so inspiring, but I'm going to attempt it. Keep reading because it will be stranger than fiction.

Thomas Merton was born in southern France in 1915. His father, a New Zealander, and his mother, an American, were both artists.

He lived in Paris, Bermuda, England and the West Indies. He was educated in France, in an English private school, at Cambridge, and after his father's death, in New York. He eventually became a Catholic and then a monk in the Trappist Order.

He died tragically when he was electrocuted in a shower. He had been a poet, a writer, a novelist, a lecturer, and the man who had inspired the Kennedys, the Berrigans, Joan Baez, Dylan, the Anti-Vietnam War Crusade, and probably the Second Vatican Council.

In between, he fell in love twice, fathered a child outside of marriage, became the most influential spiritual writer of his age, and left his community to live the even more austere life of a hermit.

With a life like that you'd expect him to be proud of his life and yet at the end of his days he would say: 'I am nobody's answer – not even my own.'

Merton's early life set the stage for the confusion of his later life. Owen Merton and Ruth Jenkins had two sons, Thomas and John Paul. Owen, the father, was Church of England whose family hated Catholics, Jews and foreigners. Ruth, his mother, came from an Episcopalian background and eventually became a Quaker. She was a pacifist but always remained distant and cold. She died when Merton was a mere child.

His father was a novelist. After Ruth died he became the lover of Evelyn Scott, the novelist. Young Thomas objected to the tussle for his father's love but he always remained fond of and extremely close to his father. But his father died when Thomas was 16.

After that young Thomas went to Cambridge. He lived a wild life there. He had many affairs and as a result of one of them a child was born. Merton initially took his responsibility seriously but lost contact with the mother and his son when he went back to America.

It is thought that both the mother and son died in an air raid during the war in London. However, Merton was never sure. He tried to find both of them later in life. He left royalties from his many books to his son and the boy's mother just in case they should be found.

In his early 20s he was not religious but went to teach at a Catholic school. There he came under the influence of a famous philosopher, James Walsh. Walsh it was who taught him to harness his genius. He brought him for weekends to a monastery in Gethsemani, Kentucky.

Having sowed his wild oats, Thomas decided that the monastery life was for him. At 27 he gave up everything and joined the monks in Gethsemani on 10 December 1941. For the next 27 years he wrestled with his vocation. He was never sure if he had made the right decision.

From the monastery he wrote one of the literary and religious classics of the century, *The Seven Storey Mountain*, which is the story of his own faith journey.

He was not afraid of humanity. Nor was he afraid of love. He criticised the awful sterility of those who, claiming to love God, have in reality dispensed themselves from the obligation to love anyone.

Two years before he died he was a patient in a hospital in Louisville. There he fell madly in love with a nurse who was half his age.

He died on 10 December 1968, the same date he'd entered the monastery in 1941. It was also the year his friends Bobby Kennedy and Martin Luther King were assassinated.

Merton had foretold his own death. Two years before he died he wrote about a dream he had. In the dream he was looking down on a wide bay as he faded out of life.

When his possessions came back to America after his tragic

electrocution, some of his friends found his camera. The last picture that Merton took was from the window of his room. When the picture was developed it was in every detail exactly as Merton had described the place of his death in his dream two years previously.

Everyone in the Merton family died young and tragically. Ruth died from cancer of the stomach, his father from a brain tumour. His brother John Paul died in the war as a young airman. His first lover and his son died as a result of an air raid, Thomas himself of electrocution at the height of his career. There are no children, no survivors.

The nurse who changed his life and taught him the real meaning of true love heard about his death on the car radio as she drove home alone from work. There was nobody to share her pain.

This is my favourite prayer which I say every day of my life. It was written by Thomas Merton:

My Lord God, I have no idea where I am going.
I do not see the road ahead of me.
I cannot know for certain where it will end.
Nor do I really know my own self,
and the fact that I think I am following your will
does not necessarily mean that I am
actually doing so.
But I believe that the desire to please you
does in fact please you
and I hope I have that desire in everything that I do.
I hope that I will never do anything apart from that desire.
And I know that if I do this
you will lead me by the right road
even though I may know nothing about it.
Therefore I will trust you always.
Even though I may seem to be lost and in the shadow of death
I will fear no evil, for you are ever with me
and you will never leave me to face my peril alone.

PART TWO

The crisis in the church

The Catholic Church in Ireland

It's time to reflect on where we are in the Catholic Church in Ireland. Specifically, Rome's influence for good or bad needs to be examined.

It is obvious that the so-called leadership (senior clerics and bishops) in Ireland is in disarray. For a time it was perceived that Diarmuid Martin was the real leader who was the ruthless voice of the church's civil service in Rome. Then he too was let down by decisions in the Vatican – showing that the church will discard anyone, even bishops and children, to protect its own power.

Cardinal Brady is attempting the impossible by occasionally agreeing with Diarmuid Martin in public whilst at the same time holding the rest of the senior clerics here together by appearing to support them too. It's not working and it is time for him to show real leadership on behalf of the whole Irish church, but especially the disillusioned believing Catholics.

They are angry, confused and lost. They have every right to be, because the clerical church has told lies, protected criminals and is so morally bankrupt that they couldn't even recognise blatant sinfulness of the worst kind.

The clerical church is falling apart (a very positive sign) because they cannot cope with 'one of their own' taking them on in public. Perceived disloyalty is the ultimate crime for the careerist cleric. Diarmuid Martin knows he has the support of most people in his efforts to finally clean up the arrogance of the past, but is criticised for needlessly humiliating his colleagues in such a public way.

The result is that many bishops are discovering for the first time what most of us know from bitter experience – the institution in Rome has to be preserved at all costs. Individuals, whether they happen to be the victims of abuse, priests or bishops, will be sacrificed to make sure the institution survives.

To be fair, some progress on behalf of the survivors of abuse has been made. But beware of making too much of it. Survivors have welcomed the resignation of some bishops. Yet those who reflect must recognise that the hierarchical Catholic Church is just as ruthless as it always has been. Institutions protect themselves at all costs. Individuals and victims were, and still are, disposable. Long live big brother.

At this point we know that some bishops can be forced out of office, yet in reality the change is at best peripheral. The might of the Vatican continues to quash the individual without any radical change in its own structures. The difference is that we now know those are the very structures which need to be demolished, because they are at the root of the dysfunction. A reader wrote to me recently saying: 'Why does Rome think it can provide the answer when we know it is part of the problem?'

It is a mistake to conclude (as the media often does) that the sexual abuse of children by priests and religious has its roots only in bad management. Nor is institutional hypocrisy the only cause of this systemic sexual abuse of children – though undoubtedly it did enable abusers to continue their criminal acts.

At the heart of the problem is a more deep-seated malaise. A combination of bad theology, the dysfunctional abuse of power and a warped view of sexuality, have contributed to what the Murphy Report repeatedly refers to as 'the systemic failure' to protect the most innocent and the most vulnerable children.

I believe that the evil clerical culture which pervades our institution, right up to the Vatican bureaucracy itself, needs to be dismantled. This present crisis may not be all bad. If we are humble enough to ask for help, it can still offer us the opportunity to become a church based on gospel values – helping the poor, encouraging the sinner, walking with the powerless, welcoming failure and finding new life in the passion of suffering.

The bad theology comes from 40 years of rejection of the principles of the Second Vatican Council. Pope John Paul II and Cardinal Ratzinger, now Pope Benedict, must accept most of the blame for stifling God's Holy Spirit.

The real issue was partially addressed by Diarmuid Martin in one of his messages. He spoke of a 'false understanding of the place of the priest in the church' and 'a totally impoverished understanding of the church as a community of the baptised.' He's absolutely correct in what he says, but, sadly, we all know that nothing is likely to change.

If we were serious, passing on real power to committed believers, an end to compulsory celibacy, accepting women priests, blessings for people in good conscience living in second relationships, new forms of the sacrament of reconciliation allowing for general absolution, an end to treating women as second class citizens, an admission that few Catholics live out the principles of *HumanaeVitae*, compassion for gay people who want to live a spiritual life, a real voice for people in choosing their priests and their bishops and, critically, a limited term of office for both priests and bishops, would form some part of the agenda for change.

We must remember that it wasn't just a few Irish bishops who made mistakes. The scandal is that it was a deliberate worldwide practice to cover up crime and sin. In the United States of America, in Australia, in Britain and, more recently, in Italy the Pope's home territory, the culture of secrecy, of failure to take responsibility to help victims, was church practice.

Too many, who should have known better, were too cowardly to stand up to autocratic and hopelessly inadequate bishops and cardinals. Too many are still afraid to stand against the Roman centralisation policy about to be foisted upon us.

This is symptomatic of an institution which has lost its way and which has little or no connection with anything for which Christ died.

A power-hungry institution which claims to be answerable to God alone, yet which persistently and deliberately acts in a sinful and criminal way, needs to be radically reformed. Re-arranging bishops on a board is simply too pathetic to take seriously.

Perhaps those in Rome don't realise how rightfully angry we are. The Vatican has shown no signs whatever of the kind of repentance and honesty required to make leadership credible. The utter arrogance shown to the Murphy inquiry is a case in point. Furthermore, the Vatican appointed the bishops it is now publicly humiliating. The kind of person they sought out to become bishops and then imposed on us failed to do all in their power to protect children because the system discouraged honesty. In short, it is Rome itself which needs to repent and reform.

A visitation from on high will add fuel to our anger unless it realises that the Catholic Church on its own is incapable of doing what is right in the matter of child abuse. Don't forget that we clerics spent fifteen years attempting to get it right, yet it took the Ferns, Ryan and Murphy reports to spell out even the most basic principles. Even now, many clerics still don't get it. Unless the Pope is humble enough to accept an inquiry into the Vatican's own procedures, he will not be taken seriously.

It is ten years since I first wrote that covering up was part of the Vatican's policy. 'Part of the human structure of the church is rotten to the core' is what I said then and still believe. No amount of wriggling will convince us that those in Rome are acting in an open and honest way even now.

One of the major problems ordinary believers have is a massive collapse in trust. Good people trusted the clerical church, and the Pope in particular. They now know that the clerical church, and perhaps even the Pope, were not trustworthy in this area.

As we know it is impossible to repair trust once it is broken so deliberately and painfully. Perhaps it may be possible to attempt to build a new relationship. That will demand a different way of being church. It cries out for a true sharing of visions and futures. But it cannot be built on the discredited structures we now have. The end has come for autocratic, hierarchical rulers answerable to no one. The game's up. It's time to make an opportunity out of a crisis.

We clergy have caused the crisis, but God's people can make it a blessing. As a church, we need to be more humble and to stop being so righteous. We need reform from the top. We should take less notice of the Vatican and more notice of the Parish Council. There is hope; there is a future, but it will not be found within the present structures nor with the present leadership.

The whole truth ...

It is easy to understand why victims of clerical sexual abuse are in despair. The clerical mindset has changed not at all, it seems.

What matters in preventing the sexual abuse of children is that we live in truth. How did it happen that every single clerical structure was lined up against the victims who had been raped, buggered and sexually abused by priests and religious? How could a church, which deals in morality, fail to see how utterly immoral and indefensible that is in the eyes of God and in the eyes of decent people.

That's the issue and that's the only issue here.

How can we own up, confess, make reparation and repent in a way which will be meaningful to people, especailly victims?

Of course, Archbishop Martin is trying to do things properly. That's his duty and it would be criminal if he didn't. Give him credit for seeing the obvious.

We want the thousands of miserable people, whose lives have been destroyed by clerical sexual abuse, to have, by some miracle, a normal life again.

Cover-up has been attempted by princes of the church all over the world. We have seen what has happened to Cardinal Law. He was found out. His people and priests turned on him, yet Rome gave him a comfortable job.

There are times when, as well as a hierarchy of clerics, there is a hierarchy of justice as well.

Justice must be seen to be done for little children who had their trust betrayed; whose relationship with God is flawed for the rest of their lives by the evil deeds of these predators; who were not protected by people who should have known better, whose bright legal minds couldn't see that innocent children must have the primary right to justice.

Legal advice in these matters is precisely what it says, legal advice. It is not moral advice, it doesn't take into account pastoral practice, and it takes no account at all of what God wants us to do. It's the lowest form of advice for the highest cost. It has left the church in a complete mess and I'm afraid the events of these past few years have done nothing to give me confidence that the church has learned anything at all.

I've been convinced for some time that the problem begins but doesn't end in Rome. It always has. That's the bitter truth which very few are prepared to face. There are many decent bishops and many decent priests who feel betrayed. But don't feel any sympathy for us. We're not innocent children who were buggered and battered by people who pretended to be men of God. Rome protects those men before helping their victims.

It all demands a new way of being church. Clerical sexual abuse is the most obvious symptom of a dying clericalism. God is asking us to have a new way of being church and a new way of being priests. We cannot hold onto the clerical club and the clerical structures and the clerical bullying and hope to regain credibility.

And we don't deserve to.

We should put our trust in God and not in lawyers.

The Ryan Report

The Ryan Report has been published and it should at last destroy every myth about the Catholic Church's contribution to the Irish State.

It is without doubt a damning report, based on fact. It is an unequivocal condemnation of religious life over a 60-year period. Priests, brothers and nuns were supposed to dedicate their lives to God and to look after the most vulnerable in society. In fact they were involved in a 'chronic systematic and all-embracing' regime abusing children physically, sexually and emotionally.

The Department of Education, which had the duty to protect children, not only ignored this systematic abuse of the most vulnerable in society, but paid religious to carry it out on their behalf.

The 1916 Proclamation speaks of cherishing all our children equally. The gospel tells us that we should become like little children if we are to be part of God's kingdom. It would be better to have a millstone hung around your neck and be thrown into the sea, than to deliberately harm one of God's little ones.

Yet in hundreds of schools, thousands of young people, particularly the poorest and most vulnerable, were routinely abused.

The report tells us that there was adequate money given to both feed and clothe these children. Many of the congregations were touting for pupils so that they could make money on them.

These children weren't criminals. Only a small proportion of them were sent there for petty offences. It is estimated that 70% of them came from two-parent families who couldn't look after their children because of poverty or alcohol abuse.

The report also tells us that leaders in the congregations and the church in general knew there was routine sex abuse of children and viewed it as a moral problem, not a crime.

'Children lived in daily terror of being beaten,' Ryan writes. Corporal punishment was, 'Pervasive, arbitrary and unpredictable ... Children lived with the daily terror of not knowing where the next beating was coming from.'

Is that the legacy of religious life in Ireland?

It is easy and correct to say that there were many good religious in these institutions and that there were many people who came through the institutions unscathed. But Ryan rightly adds that it doesn't account for the undeniable fact that children were scandalously, criminally, routinely and brutally abused by people who did it in the name of God.

It wasn't just one congregation nor was it men only. True, the report indicates that there was less sexual abuse in institutions run by women. But it does say that they were underfed, poorly looked after and used as fodder to make money.

As a result of the industrial schools, one third of those who went to them left the country as soon as they got out, and never came back. Those poor children were deprived of their family, of love, of a chance in life, of their homeland and ultimately of a chance to know a loving God.

The more I read of the report the sadder I become. It is one of the reasons why religious life, priesthood and the church as we know it, will fade from Irish society. Only then will we be able to establish some kind of believable religious life based on love, self sacrifice and spirituality.

It seems that too often in the past it has been based on bullying, brutality and greed. As a member of a religious Order myself, I am disgusted and angry. May God forgive us and may those who suffered through it find some peace and a chance to find the decent life we deprived them of.

Abuse worldwide

I make no apologies for coming back to the Ryan Report. The letters told me that this report is different. It will not be a one-week wonder. The half-hearted apologies of church leaders rang hollow.

This report is getting to the heart of the matter in people's minds. One simple fact is emerging. Abuse, brutality, dysfunctional sexuality are so deeply ingrained in the institutional church that, in peoples' minds, we cannot be trusted. We cannot be trusted to tell the truth, until it is dragged out of us; we cannot be trusted to put things right because the structure itself and those running it are incapable of discerning what is right and just. Many of us clerics are out of touch with the real world. We cannot be trusted to help the most vulnerable and we cannot be trusted with children.

Like it or not, that's the way it is. Until now, it seemed it was the bishops who were incapable of reform. Now we know that the leaders of some religious orders were just as arrogant and out of touch.

Reports from all over the world came to the same conclusion. The report into the sexual abuse by clergy of the Archdiocese of Dublin will be the last straw. It will become obvious that there must be an inquiry into every diocese and every religious congregation here. Inevitably guilty priests and religious will at last be forced to leave active ministry. That will hasten the collapse of church structures as we know them. It will, with God's grace, help us re-found priesthood and ministry, built on people's need rather than on power and control.

The biggest obstacle to change is Rome itself. But I'll come back to that later.

The Catholic Church has been involved in every part of society in Ireland, particularly in the Republic. For historical reasons, the church controlled education, healthcare and the welfare systems. They did it because it was the cheapest way the State could get it done, and because they were doing it before the State was founded. The worst culprits, congregations of brothers and nuns, were directly under the control of the bishop much more than congregations of priests were.

The Ryan Report records the systemic brutalisation of children which took place. This was a sadistic world, created and sustained by the Roman Catholic Church. Helpless children were taken away from their families. The court system judged these places of torture to be safer than their homes. These children were trapped. And then they were raped, beaten, molested, starved and bullied by men and women who took vows to serve the poorest of the poor in the name of Christ's love.

That is what makes the whole system so utterly hypocritical.

Ryan needs to be put in the context of the Catholic world it reports on. There have been at least 20 reports worldwide into abuse by priests and religious, mainly in America, Canada, Africa and Britain. All of them highlight remarkably similar forms of abuse.

These reports, taken as a whole, unlock the secret doors of sexual and physical abuse which was part and parcel of the clerical church all over the world. It was vicious, systemic and was not accidental. It was known by church authorities who turned a blind eye to this cruelty. It is clear that Pope John Paul II, local bishops and religious superiors have been aware of this culture of abuse for decades and did nothing about it. We were told, that 'holy mother church knows best.' Now we know that the church was certainly not holy and was a particularly cruel, vicious mother.

The reaction to revelations of abuse worldwide has been predictable too. Denial, a tendency to minimise, to shift blame, make a qualified apology and promise that it won't happen again. They claim it's only a minority of religious who were involved in cruel abuse. But Ryan says that too many of what we call 'good' priests and religious were aware of the evil their colleagues were perpetrating, and simply ignored it. Very few had the guts to stand up to it. At the eleventh hour, the more politically minded clerics now issue words of condemnation not because they believe it, but because they see it as the politically correct thing to do.

It's twelve years ago since I first wrote here that the church was incapable of dealing with the abuse of children in its many forms. Every report, and every scandal since, has made me more convinced of that fact. There is something radically wrong with the institutional Catholic Church. It is based on the dysfunctional foundation of clericalism – a clericalism which has nothing to do with the church Christ founded. That's the unpalatable fact that will not be faced.

Clerical culture needs to be fearlessly dismantled. It has, for centuries strangled the Holy Spirit. We need to be cleansed from the toxic controls of clericalism. We need leaders who will make decisions for the people of Ireland, and not for Rome's approval. We need radical reform of church structures and an open discussion on the nature of priesthood.

For a start, men and women, married and celibate, should be given the opportunity to serve the church. Just ignore what hits the fan, and get on with it.

Marcial Maciel Degollado

Recently a young man Raul Gonzalez, who was born in Mexico in 1980, discovered that he was the son of Fr Marcial Maciel Degollado, who was the hypocritical founder of a religious congregation now under investigation by the Vatican – The Legionaries of Christ.

For most of his life Degollado was highly respected by everyone in the Vatican, especially Pope John Paul II, who went out of his way to proclaim him as a model of spirituality for younger people. He did that even though it's now clear the Pope must have known about Degollado's double life.

The present Pope, when he was Cardinal Ratzinger, investigated this man and in fairness began to see what a ruthless abuser he was. But it seems that Pope John Paul II refused to believe Ratzinger. As soon as Ratzinger became Pope, he effectively silenced Maciel Degollado, who died a few years later in 2008.

It is now clear that Maciel had long-term relationships with at least two women on two different continents. Both of them bore him children. Even worse, the allegation is that he also raped and abused his own children. Furthermore, for years members of his own order and former members tried to get the Vatican to accept that he had also seriously abused them whilst they were young students. Of course, Pope John Paul II refused to listen. It is only now that the true picture of his abuse and rape of innocent children on many continents has emerged.

Raul Gonzalez has been telling of the dreadful life he and his brother Omar, who is 33, had as a result of Maciel's abuse. Raul was Maciel's son with Blanca Gutierrez Lara. She was 22 and Maciel was 60 when Raul was born. Maciel provided her with a home and support in Mexico. Omar was her son from a previous relationship. They knew Maciel as their father but to them he was Raul Rivas who visited them in Mexico every four months. Maciel told Blanca that he was a CIA agent and had to act secretly. He and Blanca had another son, Christian, in 1991. The family lived comfortably on the money that was sent to them by 'Senor Raul'. They never discovered he was a priest or head of a Religious

Congregation, and not a CIA agent until 1997 when the ex-seminarians accused him of abuse and his cover was blown.

When Raul Gonzalez was seven, his father, the priest, brought him on a visit to Colombia and attempted to have sex with him. When he was nine Maciel asked Blanca if she would allow Raul to come to Rome on a holiday. His father met him at the airport in a blue Mercedes. He took him to an apartment there and introduced him to three women whom he called Raul's aunts and a young girl whom he introduced as Raul's sister. His little sister was Normita and her mother was Norma Banos who was Maciel's second common-law wife and lived in Spain.

Maciel brought him to the Vatican and introduced him to Pope John Paul II. They attended the Pope's Mass there. The Pope shook hands with them and blessed them. Each morning Maciel left them, presumably to go to his office as head of the religious order and each night came back home. Raul recalls that his constant advice to all his children was, 'Don't forget to go to Mass and don't lie.'

The first rumours of Maciel as a child abuser came in the late 80s. A former member of the order, Juan Baca, wrote a letter to Pope John Paul in 1989. He explained what Maciel had done and asked the Pope that he himself, i.e. Juan Baca, could be dispensed from his priestly vows. If John Paul II had acted then, Raul and all of the others who allege abuse could have been saved. But John Paul II didn't act. Baca had told the Pope that he had been repeatedly abused by Maciel in Spain from the age of twelve right through his adolescence in Rome. He knew of at least 20 other Maciel victims. Juan Baca sent the letter in a diplomatic pouch to make sure the Pope got it. They were ignored for at least 10 years and weren't fully investigated until Ratzinger did so in 2004.

As is well known, some of the leading cardinals in Rome were on the payroll of Maciel and he had an undue influence because of that.

Meanwhile everyone entering the Legionaries of Christ learned in great detail about the 'heroically virtuous life' Maciel lived. The conspiracy of silence was maintained because every member of the order took a vow never to speak badly of their superior.

It's so sick it's hard to believe.

When the allegations first seeped into the media, religious newspapers owned by the Legionaries of Christ denounced the accusers as people who were conducting 'A conspiracy of evil' against Fr Maciel.

Raul Gonzalez says that he was ten when Maciel abused him in Madrid in 1989. In a recent interview he gave detailed information of that abuse.

After his 10th birthday Maciel arranged to send Raul to Dublin to attend a private school and to learn English.

When Gonzalez was studying in Dublin, Maciel used to bring him to London. He took him to his hotel and showed him hard-core pornography to arouse and then abuse him. After two years studying in Dublin, Gonzalez returned to his home in Mexico when the abuse became regular. Gonzalez says, 'All the days that we stayed with my dad, on every trip, there were abuses.'

Maciel would claim his leg was in pain, asking the boy to touch him comfortingly and then massage him. This led to masturbation. It was the same account of abuse as was given by many of the young seminarians. Maciel even told the seminarians that he 'had permission from Pope Pius XII for sexual relief because of his pain'.

By 1998 young Raul Gonzalez sank into a depression. Maciel arranged psychiatric treatment for him.

It seems that it was partly because of the psychiatric help that he finally resisted the sexual advances of his father whom he now knew to be a powerful priest in Rome who was a close personal friend of Pope John Paul II.

He learned of his father's death in 2008 from the TV news while sitting in his home.

In 2009 Normita's existence too became public knowledge.

Last year the new leaders of the Legionaries of Christ began to make contact with some of the many people their former founder abused repeatedly and brutally over a period of many decades.

Raul Gonzalez, and the others who were abused, are disgusted with the way the case of Maciel Degollado was handled by a succession of Popes. Allegations of improper activity were first made in the late 50s to Pope Pius XII who did, in fact, act on them. But because Maciel had contacts with extremely wealthy people all over the world he was able to buy his way into a position of influence in the Vatican once again.

The one who should have acted and didn't was Pope John Paul II and it will, and should, stand against him in the mad rush to have him beatified and even canonised.

Raul Gonzalez, while appreciating the work of Cardinal Ratzinger now Pope Benedict, refuses to let him off the hook either. He says, 'Pope Benedict in 2006 ordered my father, my daddy, Marcial Maciel to rest and to pray. Why didn't he bring him to jail?'

That's a very good question. And it is one many cardinals and indeed the Pope himself will have to answer sooner rather than later.

The Dublin/Murphy Report

The long-awaited Murphy Report on child sex abuse by priests in the Dublin Diocese has finally been published, in an edited form. Even though we had been repeatedly warned that the contents would shock us, I still found myself being physically sick as I listened to the litany of abuse by priests. The sheer brutality of these evil, clerical maniacs is beyond both belief and explanation.

How could they pretend to be priests and then repeatedly groom, rape and abuse innocent boys and girls?

How could they continue to celebrate Mass, hear confessions, visit the sick, say prayers, bury the dead, marry loving couples and generally act out 'holy' rituals, whilst at the same time planning to get their dirty sexual kicks by destroying beautiful, trusting children for life? Is there no limit to hypocrisy?

How could their warped minds live with such personal depravity? They could not have lived in denial all the time. In the quiet of the night they must have known the pre-meditated evil they were planning, otherwise conscience means nothing. Or did their consciences too disappear down the plughole of their sick selfishness?

For the first time, I'm beginning to understand why so many good people walk away from the Catholic Church. What else is there to do when, at the very highest level, that same church cultivated, educated and then protected the most heinous, evil, depraved criminals imaginable?

In these bad times I wouldn't blame people if they didn't read or listen to Judge Murphy's excellent, though terribly disturbing, report. There is only so much misery we can take. And this is misery at its most soul-destroying.

But for the sake of the children, please take the report seriously.

For decades church leaders put the survival of their little institution ahead of the integrity of children. No such institution deserves respect; nor should it be allowed to survive.

What the Murphy Report clearly implies is that the cover-up was systemic. Hypocrisy was at the heart of the Catholic Church's structures.

The Papal Nuncio's attitude to the enquiry shows where true loyalty lies. His inability to co-operate was both arrogant and un-justifiable. Rome's excuse that the wrong diplomatic channel was used is proof that the same smart-ass legalism which protected abusers, has not changed. They cannot be trusted.

The Papal Nuncio is the Pope's representative in Ireland. As a diplomat he's immune from criminal prosecution, but he is not above the law. He has a moral duty to assist the State in its attempt to uncover and punish sex-abusing criminals hiding behind the priesthood.

Across the world reports into child sex abuse in the Catholic Church all indicate that the Vatican did know about hundreds of sex-abusing priests actively preying on children. They deliberately ignored the problem and thereby caused further abuse to child-ren. The 'good' name of the church was judged more important than the protection of the innocent. Every report came to the same conclusion. This has to eat at the heart of the church's credibility.

Cardinals who protected the church and not children were promoted to Roman Offices. No wonder many historians judge this to be the biggest crisis in the church since the Reformation.

In fairness, there has been change on the ground. Children are better protected now. Diarmuid Martin, Eamonn Walsh and others have made a difference, albeit fifteen years too late. But children are safer, principally because of the perseverance of survivors who were abused and because the State belatedly took its oblig-ation to protect the vulnerable seriously.

The leaders of the Catholic Church, I'm afraid, forever stand condemned.

Letter from a wise man

Here's another letter with a different point of view:

It has been rather scarifying what has come out of the Murphy report. Even more troubling is the hierarchical response ... yes, and right up to the Pope. What I fail to understand is why did the 'good priests' stay silent. And they did, with few exceptions, like yourself.

Why didn't the good priests band together, march on bishops/Archbishop's house *en masse*, hold a silent pilgrimage of prayer in solidarity with those who suffered, stand up and be counted like Jesus did?

This is my biggest hurt – our spiritual leaders, i.e. our priests, did not lead and did not show the moral courage they demand of us in all the daily struggles we have.

There were few 'followers of Christ' among the 'good priests' in that respect. You and a very few others put yourselves on the line about this, from a long time back. But where were your brothers in Christ to stand with you?

Never mind the bishops – I think the question of the passive footsoldiers is an even bigger issue to be addressed. And if there was a Nuremburg for child abuse in Ireland, there would be many of them in the dock.

Apathy is not your drink of choice, Brian, and thanks be to God for that – you make a difference, and it's tough, but you're built cussed. So keep going and don't disappoint yourself.
(B.G., *Mayo*)

Cardinal Seán Brady

As I write, I've just been interviewed for the tenth time today about Cardinal Seán Brady's decision not to resign as head of the Catholic Church in Ireland. Isn't that a strange way of putting it? His 'decision not to resign'. That's how it was put to me. It tells me that the mass media were surprised he didn't resign.

They thought he'd get out when the going was good with a reasonable reputation intact. His health wasn't good; he was over seventy; he was caught up in a storm only partially of his own making. They were expecting him to adopt the 'I'll sacrifice myself for the good of the church' attitude. Aren't politicians the only people who hang on to the trimmings of power?

I suspect some of the media had the 'good priest, humble man of the people' tributes ready to run.

But that's not how church politics work.

Maybe it's because I'm part of the church set-up (kind of) that I wasn't in the least surprised Seán Brady stayed on. All the signs were that the cardinal was going nowhere. It didn't matter what the media, public opinion or the survivors said, the clerics are still in charge of their church.

According to that view, Seán Brady did what most other priests in the church of the time would have done. Obey the bishop and ask no questions. Keep your opinions to yourself. That's what loyalty is all about.

So why should he resign? If Seán Brady went, then who could stay? Let's stick together on this one. It's time to stop running. We'll show them how the church works. Make the announcement. Leave it at that. They'll get over it and the 'good' people (even though they are old and grey) will turn up next Sunday. We'll marry and bury them. And don't forget, they need our schools.

But what about the evil things that Brendan Smyth did, I hear you ask. What about the dozens of victims whose lives were destroyed by him? Could their lives not have been saved if the bishop and the Norbertine Order and the gardaí and everyone who knew about it, including Seán Brady, had spoken to one another and acted like adults should?

How much experience was needed to realise that two little children who were abused by a priest needed help and protection? Was it right that when they and their parents were brave enough to do something about it, the children were asked by a Doctor of Canon Law, on behalf of his bishop, to explain in detail how a sexual deviant destroyed them? (And we all know how impossible it is for abused children to talk about it.) Then they were ordered to keep the meeting a secret; they must never ever tell anyone about what took place, unless the Pope himself allowed them.

I can understand that in 1975 we clergy were so detached from reality and so dysfunctional emotionally that we might have stayed silent and thought it better to do nothing to help the little children. But when do we grow up? Do some of us still not realise how utterly indefensible such behaviour was and is? It's no wonder that the Murphy Report could make sense of such despicable behaviour only by putting it down to a systemic failure within the whole clerical church.

That means we have no choice but to change the system which failed the children and the whole church. Rather than maintaining the *status quo*, we should actively pursue change at the deepest level – and the highest level too.

That's why I am so frustrated. I see no sign of the reform and renewal which is so evidently needed. It's not just Irish clerics who 'don't get it'. It's systemic failure. And the system failure goes to head office.

Seán Brady is a decent man. Those who insist he hold on to power are also good people. The abused are brave people who must assuredly have God on their side.

We should be able to live in Christian community and journey together. Yet now the clerical church is pitted against the vulnerable and the lost. There seems to be no common ground left. It's seen as a power struggle. What a shame. What a failure.

We should be humbly listening, understanding, forgiving and coming together in reconciliation.

All the energy of this clerical ghetto, which is a total of 3% of the church, is wasted on clinging to useless, destructive power. We sustain a culture which destroys the work of the Spirit. We have become swamped in the abuse scandals – which are of our own making and which will not go away. It's not just about riding out a storm.

Can we not just admit that putting structures in place to protect children is the very least we should do but that it is not nearly enough? It's not a plan for the future of the church. Is any church leader interested in genuine reform and renewal? Will you or I ever again waken up to a story about the greatness of Jesus Christ's love, instead of being forever embarrassed by yet another scandal?

I'm frustrated that we clerics, for the most part, still cannot let go of the absolute power which has corrupted us absolutely. Can we become humble enough to learn from the abuse survivors? Can we let God's Spirit open us to the wonderful possibilities of service to a community which, despite all our failings, is still waiting for a word of hope?

A Catholic Mother

Sometimes a letter says it all. Here's a good example. It sums up the anger, the disillusionment as well as the enduring faith of so many Catholics.

I am a mother with children including teenagers and, like everyone of my generation, I came from a very strong Catholic background, a close big family, a small farm of land that we all worked on. We were not well off but there was always food on the table. Prayers after breakfast and the rosary with all the family after tea were part of our life. Lent was about going to Mass before school, prayer again at night and giving up sweets which were a treat anyway, and putting the few pence in the Trócaire box.

Memories from your childhood stay with you all your life. Catholic clergy need to understand why I and the ordinary people are angry and disgusted at the church. The priest was totally trusted by children and parents yet the church did not inform them when these abusing priests were not trustworthy.

The priest was revered by all. He got total access without question by anyone to children at school, at home and in the wider community. If he asked for a child to do work for him, parents automatically sent their child to do a good deed for the priest. No one questioned the priest. That was the power the Catholic Church had over the people. The priest's words were the words of Christ and nobody went against the priest.

I watched the priest at morning Mass slamming his fist on the pulpit, shouting at the top of his voice, telling us that we were damned and unless we repented and prayed we were going to hell. I listened to sermons on how sinful abortion was but also how single mothers were a disgrace to their families, and saw how they were shunned as unclean, but not the men involved. I watched my parents struggle to get the money together to put into the weekly church collection envelopes, afraid not to have it, as the newsletter detailed each family's contributions, and enduring the shame of not being able to donate to God's good work.

I was in a happy, secure home with parents who told us 'God is love, not hell', and went to bed at night safe, with laughter ringing in the house.

But the most vulnerable children did not have that protection and were allowed to be preyed upon by a church which used legal protection and manipulation of state and gardaí to hide from its responsibilities ...

As a young adult I travelled widely and worked with people of many religions and beliefs and was always proud to say I was an Irish Catholic. Wherever I lived I found the local church to attend Mass. But then I met two victims of abuse who told me they were not believed by their parents because priests told their parents the children were lying. I saw the pain in their eyes as they recounted the loneliness and isolation from their families with whom they had no contact any more. I listened to them talk about alcohol and drug abuse problems, their way of getting away from the pain.

These were ordinary Irish people, living in a foreign land and they were not looking for money but someone to listen and believe them and help them out of the darkness they were in.

I was completely shocked, totally unqualified to deal with their problems, but I was an ear and I believed them. I never knew what happened to these people but have never forgotten them. Never again did I take for granted that priests lived the moral life they preached from the altar.

I have met many wonderful priests who work hard for their church and parish and it is tough for them too as they watch their church and beliefs being torn apart because of a few, and the revelations of cover-up by their bishops ...

How dare the bishops preach morals at confirmations to our children on the altar, and then stand idly by and do nothing for abused children?

Cardinal Brady had a Doctorate in Canon Law. Was he there at the children's interviews as a lawyer for the church? What I find most interesting is that Canon Law stated that bishops are there to defend the priests' rights. So who was there to defend the children? Surely the church realised it was against all moral codes to abuse, and facilitate the continued abuse of a child, male or female.

The church put guidelines in place in 1996 but the abuse was going on for over 40 years. I want to know why it took so long putting these in place, when they knew for decades about clerical abuse.

I am a mother and I am outraged that even one child (never mind thousands) was raped/abused by paedophile priests and that my church covered it up.

This is not going to go away, ever, unless it is dealt with openly, by the church. No more trickling of information when forced to do so. No more publicity stunts. We see through it!

The present leaders might not have been the leaders then but they were adults and they did nothing. No amount of pleading, 'Look at what we're doing now' is going to wash with me. I do not believe you …

I have read the Pope's letter online, but where is the acknowledgment of guilt that abuse was actively covered up from Rome to Ireland? The faith of the people of Ireland was called into question. That is an insult. It was not the fault of the people. The faith of the people of Ireland is and has been strong.

The day of the Catholic clergy in Ireland telling people how to live their lives is gone. Religion has to go back to grassroots levels to survive. The people's opinion must be heard.

I am sad at the Catholic Church's demise. I now pray at home but my faith in God has never diminished.

I hope someday to go back to Mass and encourage my children to get actively involved but how can I, until I *believe* the church lives by what it preaches?

(*A Catholic mother. Name given. Sent by e-mail*)

Living in denial

The words of Archbishop Diarmuid Martin, in his talk to the Knights of St Columbanus, have been analysed repeatedly. Most of us know by now that politics within the clerical church in Ireland, and indeed in Rome, is a murky business. That is one of the reasons why Diarmuid Martin felt so frustrated.

He's right when he says that there are strong elements within the Catholic Church who still live in denial about the extent of sexual abuse. Priests in religious Orders and in dioceses still haven't taken onboard the extent to which the sexual abuse of children has destroyed trust in the church. Diarmuid Martin is not the only one who is isolated within the clerical club because of his stand against abuse and its cover-up.

Most leaders of religious Orders are experiencing the same kind of hostility when they try to protect children. The usual question is asked: 'Where has compassion gone?'

Even well educated clerics, who criticise cover-ups in the past, in practice still hold that compassion should be distributed only to the cleric and not to the survivor. It is frustrating for Diarmuid Martin and others to experience the backbiting and hostility for doing what is right. These 'strong forces' make life difficult and ensure the culture of cover-up will not go away.

Perhaps Diarmuid Martin would have been more helpful if he had named the sources of opposition. Is it found in other members of the hierarchy? Is it found with senior members of his own archdiocese? Is it lay organisations perhaps? Is it the right wing Catholic press? We need to know who it is he feels is resisting God's Holy Spirit to renew the church. That is an unforgivable sin. Such people should not be in ministry today.

He talks about 'signs of subconscious denial'. I am not so sure that it is subconscious. It takes a conscious decision to deny the extent and the scandal of abuse within the Catholic Church in Ireland.

The archbishop is right too when he highlights the seriousness of the crisis of faith we are facing in the country. Perhaps this is where he shows his inexperience in dealing with the Catholic Church in Ireland. He has spent most of his life in Rome and would not have been aware that many people have been trying to come to terms with this faith diminishment for two decades. But it is good that he has come to that conclusion and it is refreshing to hear a man in leadership recognising that there is a serious crisis of faith.

He points the finger at the Catholic education system. Again I think the question he asked is a valid one. What is a Catholic ethos in a school? How come that in a nominally Catholic school neither the majority of the pupils nor the majority of the teachers are believers?

The archbishop is right to say that in parishes there is hardly any outreach to young people. Perhaps one of the main reasons for this is the falloff in the numbers and in the quality of vocations to the priesthood. He mentioned that in his own diocese there are ten times more priests over the age of 70 than there are under the age of 40. With that profile, it would be difficult to have an outreach to youth. As long as outreach remains the responsibility of the clerics, it won't happen.

Archbishop Martin praised the role of prophets within Christian communities. Prophets will always suffer. He can console himself that he, when he deals with realities, is a prophet suffering hostility.

'The Catholic Church in Ireland in the future will have to find its place in a very different, much more secularised culture, at times even in a hostile culture,' the archbishop said.

Future generations will not learn about the church in the home or in the school, so it is up to parish communities to find ways of catechising young people. In almost every other European country and in North American, parish catechising has worked remarkably well. 'The Catholic Church in Ireland cannot be imprisoned in its past. The work of evangelisation must, if anything, take on a totally new vibrancy,' he said.

It is important to listen to what Archbishop Martin said. But I hope he goes on to answer the many questions he raised. The archbishop is frustrated, and in many ways his speech showed that. If the church belongs to all the people, he should be brave enough now to go one step further and talk in less diplomatic terms about where the problem lies.

Letter from a reader

There are many priests trying hard to hold on by their finger-tips, though not too many who are liberated enough to speak honestly. Here's the story of one young, talented man who once thought about becoming a priest.

Your energy for the voice of reason is tireless, a true gift! My story is short, but not without its complexities. I'm a 30 year old man living in Northern Ireland. Throughout all of my teenage years I had a longing to become a Catholic priest. Being brought up in a moderately Catholic home, this should not have raised many serious concerns. However, I held my aspirations between myself and God ...

The main reason I longed for priesthood was simple – I wanted others to know how good it was to be in a relationship with God. I needed to live my life in communion with God and to help people in whatever way I could, and I felt priesthood was the only viable path for me to take.

In my early twenties, I went to a vocations retreat where I met other men who appeared to be sharing some of the same feelings and questions as myself. It was a frightening time, and a very exciting time. I felt at last I was doing something about what I had been carrying with me for ten years. A visit to the national seminary followed where I met more men from all over the country. After discernment with some priests, I returned home to my parents to tell them of my decision to study for priesthood.

Their reaction was utter dismay. They asked why would I want to limit my life, mainly the chance to be in a human relationship; the chance to have children; the chance to freedom of opinion without being reprimanded. They pleaded with me to think about it for one more year before entering. I reluctantly agreed but I felt like I was being held back from something I was ready for.

Wow! What a year!

As I tried to make sense of the scripture I was reading and

attempted to apply it to my life, floods of revelations about clerical child sex abuse emerged. My heart sank. I was truly sickened and as time passed, I felt utterly betrayed by what these people had done to children, and more selfishly, to me.

That was ten years ago. I have studied scripture. I have listened to the words of many different people. I have watched the inaction of church figures. I have moved on.

Yet, my questions have never been answered and have only multiplied. Why must a priest be called 'father' when the church he belongs to denies him this basic human right? Why must bishops have their rings kissed, be given fancy titles and palaces, and be accountable to Rome but not the people whom they serve? Why was there a higher prevalence of homosexual men and sexually immature men in that seminary, than in the wider society? What kind of people are going forward for priesthood today? What are their motives? Where is Jesus' message of love for our neighbours in the lives of many church figures? Why is the Pope infallible and called 'the Holy Father' (after all, there was nothing holy or fatherly in leaving children to the wolves of paedophilia)?

People of Ireland … Stand up! Take back your church which has been hijacked by this single men's club. Make your church what it should be. Inclusive, not exclusive. Truth, not a conspiracy of lies. It is yours, take it back! If parishes want a priest, select someone whom you consider capable of the job from the community. They don't have to be celibate. They don't have to be male. They have to be human. They must also be directly accountable to their employers: the people.

I thank God for the wisdom of others who steered me well clear of priesthood. I thank those who pursue truth tirelessly. I now help people in a different way. I live my life to the full as Jesus promised. I have a brilliant woman in my life whom I will marry shortly and hopefully become a 'father' for real! I have not attended church in six years and I'm a happy man – Jesus has promised us he is with us always, even to the end of time. I believe the end of time for this Catholic Church has arrived. I'm glad I'm outside it, because it's in the clear, fresh air of freedom that God, Jesus Christ and the Holy Spirit can truly reign supreme.

All the best on your life's journey Brian (I think the absence of titles suits you better!)

James. (Not his real name and sent by e-mail).

Shame

Frequently in the letters pages of newspapers writers call on the whole church to do penance in reparation for the harm done by clerical sexual abuse of children. They make a good point. We have done nothing to make reparation for the sins of the church. Maybe we haven't fully accepted the need for penance because we live in denial. Some leaders, including Archbishop Martin and Cardinal Brady, have used the word 'shame' to describe how they feel about what happened to innocent children.

I was interested in an article by Mary Gail Frawley-O'Dea in which she outlined two kinds of shame – healthy and unhealthy. The writer is a clinical psychologist and has frequently addressed the Conference of Catholic Bishops in the United States on the sexual abuse issues. She co-edited a book called *Predatory Priests, Silenced Victims*. In other words she has experience in the field.

She writes: 'Shame is a tricky business. Shame is … not just something we did that we now regret. This evokes guilt, an emotion comparatively easily faced in comparison to shame. Shame is about who we are, not just what we did. It is usually a profoundly destabilising, emotional, physical and spiritual state; we blush, we feel sickened to the stomach in spirit, are afraid and want to hide. Too much of it can stultify growth … when shame cripples we can no longer look ourselves or our communities in the eyes. We are alone. Too many sexual abuse survivors, in fact, labour under this burden of often self destructive and always isolating shame that was never theirs to carry in the first place.'

She then goes on to describe a more healthy form of shame. 'There is a shame experience that deepens our relationships with ourselves, others and the sacred. This shame signals that we transgressed and instructs us to make amends and warns us to refrain from behaviour that leads to the deepening of shame …'

She says this healthy shame is a gift. And it is a gift that has not been fully accepted by church leaders. 'Too many bishops and other church officials have projected what should be their shame unto others – the media, attorneys, therapists and anti-Catholics – by whom the church then declares itself victimised. The oppressors subjectively experience themselves as victims and the need for penance evaporates.' She feels that the call for ecclesiastical heads to role may not always be healthy. In fact it may be an easy way out. 'The bishops go and with them the shame that is better invited into the parlours of the Vatican and Chanceries across the globe.' The answer she thinks is for the Pope to lead his bishops in creative encounters with shame, through meaningful acts of public penance:

> What if bishops worldwide substituted millstones for pectoral crosses, fashioned to be just heavy enough to remind these men of the suffering they and their brethren turned blind eyes to? Worn publicly they would also serve as icons of remembrance to other priests and Catholics who should remain vigilant about holding themselves and each other to accountability for the safety of the children of the church.
>
> What if members of the hierarchy got out of their Chanceries and spent time every month in the kitchens of survivors and their families, listening abundantly to their stories and apologising to these people of God?
>
> What if they visited the family of every victim in their diocese who committed suicide and with every victim who is in jail or rehab – and apologised on behalf of themselves and for all Catholics?
>
> What if bishops, clad in sackcloth, dedicated every First Friday to leading the Stations of the Cross in honour of victims, inviting victims and their families to be present, if they can stand being in a church or being with clergy again?

Mary Gail Frawley-O'Dea's suggestions are worth thinking about. Some bishops may need to resign, but all bishops and many of us priests need a radical change of heart to act more humbly. Stop pretending we are the victims, and experience real shame at our inability to recognise sin and crime; stop clinging to power and instead spend more time in prayer and penance for our own sins and the sins of those who still live in denial about the grave harm done to innocent children.

PART THREE

Healing our wounded church

The church then and now

I often wonder how the church I am supposed to represent came into being. I can find very little in common between today's church and the story of the first Christian communities in the Acts of Apostles. Pushers of religion rarely have any of the simple spirituality of the gospels. And it's not just the Catholic Church.

All over the world, churches come together to pray for Christian unity. Its basis is the prayer of Jesus, 'That they all may be one.' Even a furtive glance at churches around the world will show that, officially, there are few signs of unity among the major churches.

Furthermore, there is deep division within many of the churches. In Protestant churches there are fundamentalists who make God as small as their bigoted selves. The Catholic Church is divided between a shrinking clerical elite and angry lay believers who recognise they are being ignored. Many others are dismissed as 'lapsed Catholics'. I don't know what a lapsed Catholic looks like. It seems to presume that you can only be Catholic if you are perfect in every way. Once a human lapse occurs, 'you're gone'.

Jesus would never agree with that. In fact he died to make sure that imperfect people would find a home within his kingdom.

A recent survey in America showed that about 10% of all Americans are 'former Catholics'. And it has been estimated that if former Catholics were to constitute a denomination unto themselves, they would be the second largest religious group in the United States. The largest group would be the Catholic Church itself.

Anglicans are as bad as Roman Catholics for washing their dirty linen in public. Do they believe that gays and lesbians can be saved? Or do they believe that gays and lesbians should be bishops and archbishops? Do they believe in protecting life at its beginning and its end? Do they believe that it is possible to pray with Catholics and still get to heaven? What do they believe about anything? There are so many divisions within the churches that Christian Unity Week should start by praying there will be some sort unity *within* churches as well as *among* churches.

One characteristic which all churches have in common is that they are moving further and further away from the simple principles outlined in the gospel. Let me ask you a simple question. It is one I ask myself often: What has priesthood today in common with the carpenter who hung on a cross?

The late Cardinal Hume, shortly before he died, wrote a letter to the Conference of Bishops of the United States of America. He was too ill to go in person so he put it on video. It was played to the Conference of Bishops the day after he died. He pointed out to them that the civil service in Rome caused great damage because they have been given too much power. He talked about receiving letters from the Papal civil service in which he felt he was being scolded as a schoolboy might be for doing something unacceptable.

It happened especially during the reign of Pope John Paul II. Members of the curia think that it is they, along with the Pope, who run the church. Hume pointed out that it is the Pope and bishops who govern the church, not the Pope and the curia.

Without a doubt the church has been badly served by the quality of men who were appointed bishops by civil service in Rome.

With the Catholic Church in disarray all over the world, one of these curial offices, with the backing of the Pope, wants to re-impose an outdated official version of the Mass in English. From what I have seen of it, it will be a disaster. Yet bishops all over the world have caved in to bullying from the papal civil service.

At the Second Vatican Council we got away from Latin prayers. We were told that the English translations: 'should radiate a noble simplicity. They should be short, clear, free from useless repetition. They should be within the people's power of comprehension, and normally should not require much explanation.'

By and large that's why we got prayers in English that we could understand. Now the fiddlers in Rome want to re-impose what they call a *proper* Latin translation.

Much of it is incomprehensible, archaic and totally without merit. They are trying to re-impose what they call 'a sacred language.' For example in The Creed, 'Born of the Virgin Mary,' now becomes 'incarnate of the Virgin Mary'. And 'One in being with the Father', becomes 'Consubstantial with the Father.'

Here is a list of words that you won't see too often in the *Sunday World*, thank God: 'Ineffable,' 'Consubstantial,' 'Incarnate,' 'Inviolate,' 'Oblation,' 'Ignominy,' 'Precursor,' 'Suffused,' and 'Unvanquished'. Would anyone in their right mind ever use any of those words? Yet those are the words which will be imposed in our most sacred prayer – the celebration of the Mass.

It's another example of power-hungry, out-of-touch clerics destroying what's left of common sense in the church.

I used to say that I spent most of my life 'smuggling people into heaven behind the backs of bishops'. Of course I don't smuggle anybody into heaven. Jesus saves and I do whatever I can to help. I write this to let you know just how frustrating it is being a priest in today's church, and it's getting worse by the day.

Abortion

First, let me state categorically that I'm against abortion. I do not agree with those who are pro-choice, but I continue to listen and learn why they think the way they do.

I am against euthanasia yet I support the view that extraordinary means to prolong or prevent death usually cause more problems and more suffering than can be justified.

I am against the deliberate taking of human life, and that includes killing for a political principle. The death penalty makes me sick in the pit of my stomach.

I also realise at this stage of my life that whilst it is easy to promulgate principles, compassion must be at the heart of every principle.

That is why I found it impossible to understand why the Archbishop of Recife in Brazil should formally excommunicate the medical team and the mother of a nine-year-old girl for their part in an abortion performed on the little girl. She became pregnant with twins after being repeatedly raped by her stepfather.

The Archbishop, Jose Cardoso Sobrinho, justified it on the grounds that abortion was a 'silent holocaust'. I understand his need to condemn abortion, since it is estimated that one million illegal abortions take place in Brazil every year. Brazilian law officially allows abortion only in cases like rape. But formal excommunication for mother and doctors shows a horrible ignorance of the facts.

To make matters worse, a top Vatican official, Cardinal Giovanni Battisa Re, supported the Brazilian archbishop.

However, many other bishops and archbishops in the Brazilian hierarchy disagreed with their colleague in Recife and because they were in Rome, got together to express 'solidarity with this girl and with all children who are victims of such a brutal act.' They went on to say: 'The Lord's mandate, you shall not kill, must take priority.' That's not very helpful to anyone, especailly the nine-year-old victim of rape.

Medical science has shown that, had the nine-year-old girl who was so brutally raped by somebody who should have cared for her, carried the twins to full term, she would have died herself because she was not physically mature enough to carry the twins.

I cannot understand how anyone would expect a nine-year-old girl, who was brutally raped and abused, to lay down her own life, in the certainty that she and her barely formed little twins would all die together.

The medical team, who were all Catholics, after days of searching and looking for moral guidance, decided that their intention was not to kill the babies but rather to save the life of the little girl. In the end, the abortions to save the little girl's life was ordered by a Brazilian court and the doctor obeyed the court order.

The little girl herself, because she is under 16, could not be excommunicated.

Worse still, the church took no action against the stepfather who had brutally raped and assaulted this innocent little girl. Archbishop Sobrinho said: 'It is clear he committed a very serious sin, but the abortion is worse than this.'

Many Catholics in Brazil have been angered by Archbishop Sobrinho's excommunication, arguing that if the church's Law is so merciless, then it cannot be right. Many also argued that had the stepfather been excommunicated it would have shown some consistency of thought.

All is not lost just yet. At least one official in Rome, Archbishop Rino Fisichella, who heads the Vatican's Pontifical Academy for Life, has said that the doctors and the mother of the little girl did not deserve excommunication because: 'The doctors were saving the little girl's life.'

He argues that mercy and compassion should have been the key elements in the bishop's statement. Before thinking about excommunication, Archbishop Fisichella said: 'It was necessary and urgent to save the girl's innocent life and bring her back to a level of humanity of which we men of the church should be expert and masters in proclaiming.'

He went on to say that the young girl, 'Should have been above all defended, embraced, treated with sweetness, to make her feel that we were all on her side, all of us, without exception.'

He went on to stress that abortion is 'always condemned by

moral law as an intrinsically evil act'. But commenting on the hasty excommunication he added: 'Unfortunately the credibility of our teaching took a blow, as it appeared in the eyes of many to be insensitive, incomprehensible and lacking mercy ...'

A deliberate abortion automatically carries the penalty of ex-communication according to Canon Law.

In all of this I cannot help but think of the way Jesus dealt with the woman taken in adultery. The Law required that she be put to death by stoning. And when Jesus didn't enforce that Law, he was accused of setting a bad example to others. However, Jesus was willing to run that risk and instead showed compassion. He did not condone the woman's behaviour because he told her to go and sin no more.

That sort of pastoral care for the little girl would have been better appreciated. It seems to me that those who wanted to force the girl to die, so that their principles could be maintained, are not entirely without sin themselves. 'Casting the first stone ... etc.'

Thank God for Archbishop Fisichella, his compassion and his leadership. Principled, sensitive men like him will help to heal our battered church.

Staying put

President Mary Mc Aleese has a great gift for stating profound truths in a simple way. She once wrote, in a publication called *Family Matters*, this guide for believing in dark times:

> I have lived unhappily through some of the recent public controversy over church-based scandals and disputes. I have been saddened, disappointed, angered, shocked and frustrated – sometimes all in one day.
>
> But what has it meant for me, for my faith in God and for my faith in church?
>
> My faith in Christ and in the church has to be precisely that, *mine*; felt deeply in my own heart and in my own soul, linked to Christ and to Christ only. If my faith is strong only for as long as no priest commits a crime, no bishop makes a mistake, no member of the church is hypocritical or sinful, then was it ever faith in the first place?
>
> If my faith shatters because someone whom I respect or admire turns out to be a public sinner, who then was my guide? Was it Jesus Christ or was it a very human understudy?

Catholics in Britain

How do you react to this statement? 'The average Catholic in Britain today has had a Catholic education, supports Catholic schools, prays daily, attends Mass on Sunday although feels no obligation to do so. But although the average Catholic receives communion at nearly every Mass attended, he or she hardly ever goes to confession.' That, in summary, is the result of a survey carried out by the authoritative Catholic magazine, *The Tablet*. They surveyed 1,500 Catholics at parishes in England and Wales. It doesn't take into account the views of Catholics in Ireland or Scotland, but are they any different?

There is some good news in the survey, because the average practising Catholic is committed to their faith, their marriages, family and Catholic education.

Whether the church authorities acknowledge it or not, in my experience the results in *The Tablet* survey are a reasonably accurate reflection of what Catholics in Ireland believe and practise too.

Where the Church in England might differ is in the number of immigrants they have been coping with over a long number of years. But like here, Catholics from Poland and Brazil are bringing their own form of renewal to the church in Western Europe.

This survey concentrated on Catholics in the pews. Therefore, it's ordinary Catholics who still practise who were asked these questions.

It discovered that the traditional source of passing on the faith, namely the family, can no longer be relied upon. In most families both parents work and because of long days they don't have the energy or the time to have a living, on-going influence on their children. The clearest trend from the survey was that those who attend Mass regularly see themselves as being highly committed Catholics, yet a sense of obligation to attend Mass matters less and less to the younger generations.

Again in a trend away from the past, modern Catholics, when they attend Mass, wish to receive communion whether they have been to confession or not. So their sense of sin is very different to previous generations.

Further good news is that Catholics still attach a huge import-ance to marriage and family life. The modern parent, probably be-cause they have fewer children, spends almost all the free time they have with their children.

In Britain in general, where half the children of British born mothers have been born outside wedlock, marriage is still strongly supported by Catholics. Of the 18 to 35 year olds interviewed in the survey, only 13% were living with a partner while almost 50% were married. In the 36 to 45 year old bracket, only 5% were co-habiting and 72% were married.

In the area of family life, the influence of immigrant cultures was particularly evident, with far more of those from abroad say-ing they prayed at home with their families.

Amongst ethnic minorities Catholics marrying Catholics was strongest. 85% of South East Asians had a Catholic spouse, 77% of Irish and 77% of Africans had a Catholic spouse but with British born Catholics, only 64% married another Catholic.

Catholics still have an amazing respect for, and loyalty to, Catholic education. They by far prefer church-run schools.

What was most shocking to me in the report, though, was the fact that even though so many attended Catholic schools, the re-spondents had a pathetically poor knowledge of church matters. For example, a huge number of them had never heard of the Second Vatican Council. The majority had not heard of *Humanae Vitae*, the encyclical published over 40 years ago, outlawing artifi-cial contraception.

Attendance at Mass is still central to Catholic belief in England and Wales. In the 18 to 35 bracket 62% said they attended Mass at least once a week. In the 46-65 year old 84% attended Mass each week and in the over 65 group 92% did. When asked the reasons why they attended church, 64% said they wanted to express com-mitment to God and 55% felt it gave them strength to carry on every day. Only 36% attended to feel part of a community.

When it comes to prayer, 66% of the respondents said they prayed every day. South East Asians were the highest group with 85% saying they prayed every day. Of the Irish in Britain 78% said they prayed every day while 59% of the British-born prayed each day.

I also liked how respondents were asked about the importance of developing qualities in their children. The most important qualities were honesty, tolerance, good manners, unselfishness, the feeling of responsibility, faith and hard work. While the least popular were obedience, independence, imagination, volunteering, thrift and saving money. Make what you will of that, but it gave me grounds for hope.

Anne Rice

Anne Rice is one of the best-selling novelists in the world today. She has sold over 100 million books and is probably best known for her Vampire novels. She created huge media interest when she announced on her Facebook that she had, 'Quit being a Christian'. Since then she has given interviews on radio, television and to newspapers. Whilst she is adamant she has forsaken organised Christianity as she wrestles with her doubts, it is clear she still is a convinced searcher.

Her faith journey has always been public and controversial. She was born into the Catholic Church and raised on its rituals. In her early life, though, she became a convinced atheist even though culturally her novels remained Catholic.

However, in 1998 she proclaimed that she wanted to rejoin the Catholic Church. She found atheism no longer tenable and for the past twelve years she was a vociferous if struggling Catholic.

Rice has repeatedly said that she still believes in God but, 'In the name of Christ, I refuse to be anti-gay. I refuse to be anti-feminist. I refuse to be anti-birth-control. I refuse to be an anti-democrat. I refuse to be anti-science. I refuse to be anti-life.'

Rice says she wants to reject the current trend within the Catholic Church to persecute gays, and women.

'I found that I can't find a basis in scripture for a lot of the positions that churches and denominations hold today. And I can't find any basis at all for an anointed hierarchical priesthood ... this created a pressure and confusion within me ... a toxic anger at times and I felt I had to step aside.'

Some are cynically saying that it is a publicity stunt for her new books, *Of Love And Evil*, and *Angel Times*. But when you have sold over 100 million copies, who needs publicity?

It's my view that Anne Rice is putting honest words on what a lot of struggling people think about all religions, and particularly the Catholic religion, at present. For example the Lutherans invited her to join their church but she insists that in the name of God and in the name of Christ she can't find a peaceful place within any organised religious group.

She realises it will be difficult to follow Christ without being a church member. Ritual, because of her Catholic background, is important to her and so is prayer.

'I think the basic ritual is simply prayer. It's talking to God, putting things in the hands of God, trusting that you're living in God's world and praying for God's guidance. And being absolutely faithful to the core principle of Jesus' teaching.'

She says she'll miss going to Mass and she'll miss Holy Communion the most. She still loves churches and if it doesn't offend anybody she still would like to go into Catholic Churches to have a peaceful place to pray.

When she was asked what was the last straw that forced her to step aside, she admitted there was more than one last straw. When the Pope went to Africa and spoke out against the carers who promoted the use of condoms to prevent the spread of AIDS, she found his attitude utterly irresponsible and indefensible.

When the Pope went to Portugal and said, 'The most insidious evil which faced the world today was same sex marriages' she concluded, 'We live in a world where genocide and human slavery are realities and the Pope chose to focus on same sex marriages. That was a moment of "What in the world am I doing connected to this religion?"'

The attitude of some bishops in the American hierarchy was what finally pushed her over the edge. There was one incident in particular. The Bishop of Phoenix Arizona invoked an excommunication on Sr Margaret McBride, who was part of an ethics group in the local hospital. In order to save the life of a mother, the group allowed an operation which resulted in the abortion of an unborn child. Most theologians, and those involved in medical ethics, recognised it as a clear case where both the mother and child would die unless some intervention took place. The ethics committee concluded that the child on its own could not be saved, but that the mother could be saved. A secondary result of their operation was sadly the death of the unborn baby. Most thought it entirely unjust to excommunicate Sr Margaret McBride. For Anne Rice, the bishop's actions were so unjust and wrong that she could no longer be part of the same organisation as he was.

It seems to me that Anne Rice puts words on how a great number of people feel. They know that what they are being offered from the churches is neither helpful nor life-giving.

Gerry Ryan and the Sign of Peace

Many years ago when I was helping out in Africa, I attended a meeting of a group of religious people working there. We were discussing the differences between religious customs and religious cultures from various parts of the world. An African nun, who had returned from Europe, said that Europeans don't take their religion seriously. She went further and said that, since religion had become mere ritual, it would die out in time.

I took her seriously but didn't quite understand her point. She used the sign of peace at Mass as an example. At their most expressive, people shake hands and even then it's not very enthusiastic. There's no feeling, no sincerity.

'People rarely even look at each other when they are exchanging the Sign of Peace,' she concluded.

Another African woman told us that when they exchange the Sign of Peace in her local church, they first give each other a hug and say to the other person, 'I love the face of Christ I see in you.' Then they try to really experience the peace of Christ as they prepare to become one with Christ in Communion.

I tried this out when I came back from Africa. I explained the story as I have told you. I wondered if we could look at one another and say, 'I love the face of Christ I see in you.' A few children did it and the adults were so embarrassed that most of them put their hands in their pockets.

If you can't look your neighbour in the face in church today, could I ask you to consider something else?

Tomorrow morning, when you get up, whether you are a man or woman, go to the mirror and see the wrinkles in your face, notice the sagging little bags under your eyes. Try to count the chins and don't be too put off by the pale face and red eyes. Stare at yourself for five seconds and then say, 'I love the face of Christ I see in you.' If you can't say that to yourself, then how can you love anyone?

When I came home I shared the story with Gerry Ryan on his radio programme. In his usual way, he was all for the passionate greeting and often brought it up in conversations down the years.

I met him just before Christmas and once again he asked: Any progress on the face of Christ greeting? I had to admit I had long since given up and that the African nun was correct in her assessment – our liturgies are as lifeless as our beliefs.

At the end of our liturgies we usually say, 'Go in peace to love and serve the Lord.' That's my wish for you too Gerry. Go in peace and I know the Lord loves you always.

Women priests [I]

Is it possible for the Catholic Church to ordain women? That is a question many committed Catholics are asking in different parts of the world. There is a crisis in priesthood and it is not possible to have a healthy discussion about the future of the priesthood if it is restricted to male celibates only.

There already is a married priesthood. Men who joined the Anglican Church and became ministers and who disagreed with the ordination of women in the Anglican Church, have been ordained as Roman Catholic priests. They practise their priesthood as married priests.

The very best of luck to such people, but it smacks of indefensible hypocrisy. On the one hand we are told that only male celibates can be ordained, but when it suits another agenda, married men can be ordained. Yet those priests who have given their entire lives to the Catholic Church are forced to leave the priesthood if they wish to marry. That's hypocrisy.

Many theologians say that when it comes to discussing who can be ordained, we should not confine the discussion to whether it should be married or single men. They say that, in justice, at least we should discuss the possibility of whether women can/ should be ordained. Other churches, using the same scriptures as the Catholic Church, have come to the conclusion that it is possible to ordain women to the priesthood.

However, if one were to state that women should be ordained or, worse still, show solidarity with women who have claimed ordination, then as a priest one will be silenced and even excommunicated from the church altogether. That's how it is now, and it is a grave injustice to the priests and to all women who in conscience feel called by God to priesthood.

You may think I am exaggerating. Far from it. Take the case of Fr Roy Bourgeois. As a young man Roy was conscripted into the American Army and fought in Vietnam. It changed him forever. When he came out, he became a pacifist. He also joined the Maryknoll religious order and was ordained a priest nearly 40 years ago.

During his life he has campaigned for justice and, in the process, 'disturbed many a hornets' nest'. Mainly he campaigned against the United States Foreign policy in South America. Fr Roy worked for a long time in Bolivia. He saw at first hand how damaging US policy was to Latin America. His protests have been public and led to his being jailed on more than one occasion.

But of all the scary episodes in his life, the latest is the most difficult. This time it is not the United States government taking away his freedom, but the Roman Catholic Church which he has served for 40 years. He believes passionately that it is possible for women to be ordained in the Catholic Church. He says: 'Who are we, as men, to say to women, "Our call is valid but yours is not." Who are we to tamper with God's call?'

He knew his life would never be the same again when he took part in a service of 'ordination' for a long-time proponent of women's ordination, Janice Sevre-Duszynska. Almost immediately the Vatican took action against him. They said that unless he recanted within 30 days, he would be excommunicated from the Roman Catholic Church.

Not only would he be unable to act as a priest, he would not be able to call himself a member of the Catholic Church and all because he spoke in favour of the ordination of women.

When he heard the sad news, the one he worried most about was his 95-year-old father, Roy senior, a devout Catholic and daily Mass goer. Fr Roy went off to think about his future. He knew that he could never recant because he believes that if women have discerned a call from God to ordination, then that call cannot be rejected without being contrary to God's will. That's his firm conscientious conviction.

He decided that he would like to meet Pope Benedict XVI and Cardinal William Levada, head of the Congregation of the Doctrine of the Faith, face to face, so that he could explain his position.

His family were worried about Fr Roy but even more so about their 95-year-old dad. So Fr Roy went to meet his two sisters, Ann and Janet, and his brother Dan in their father's house. His sisters and brother were sure that the news would break their father's

HEALING OUR WOUNDED CHURCH 103

heart. But when they told their father that Roy would be excommunicated, Roy senior broke down and cried. Then he said: 'God brought Roy back from the war in Vietnam. God took care of Roy in his mission work in Bolivia and El Salvador, and God is going to take care of Roy now. Roy is doing the right thing by following his conscience and I support him fully.'

Then he added: 'God will look after our family too.' If only our church leaders had the wisdom of that venerable old man.

Fr Bourgeois was quoted as saying: 'When I received dad's blessing and the blessing of my family, I felt great peace. A total peace came over me. And I have felt peaceful ever since. Nothing the Vatican does will be able to take that peace and serenity away.'

After almost 40 years as an active priest, it will be difficult for him not to be a member of the Catholic Church officially. He knows it will be tough. But he knows he is being guided by the Holy Spirit and the Holy Spirit always leads faithful people to a place of Truth and Peace.

The time is here for all right-thinking Catholics to ensure the voice of hope is heard. May the Spirit of God guide us.

Women Priests [II]

Not everyone agrees with my views on the church. Thank God for that. It would be boring if they did. Here's a good letter from a man who reacted strongly to what I said about women priests.

Dear Fr Brian,
I've read your article on the possibility of ordaining women priests. I sense that you would very much like women to be ordained to the priesthood, although you don't quite clarify that view; instead you seem to clarify the Fr Roy Bourgeois view.

I'm concerned that many male priests within the Catholic Church seem only too keen to champion women being ordained to priesthood. The reason I'm concerned is that there is a real lack of men attending Mass these days. It's as if men don't matter anymore, like we've become some nuisance to the rest of the human race. Some priests say that we men need to get in touch with our feminine side. I find this disturbing because God made us men so what's wrong with being in touch with our masculine side?

I think the fact there is a fall in priestly vocations is because of the child sex abuse scandal that has rocked the church, and partly because the gospel has been watered down so much that God now appears a bit 'telly tubby' when we hear about his love. This puts men off going to Mass and some men from following the call to priesthood.

I've no doubt a woman can do all that a man can do, but if women do everything, then what's the purpose of life for a man? Is he to be made redundant? Where is your concern for your male friends? Are you going to have a go at Jesus on your judgement day because he picked 12 male apostles despite having so many women following him? Do you not think that he had a good reason for picking only men? Is it not possible that God wants men to be responsible, to take responsibility for how they exercise their life?

Instead today's men expect the woman to take all responsibility while they step back from their role. Sometimes men just sit at home after work and focus on the latest episode of the Simpsons. That's where priests come in. A priest needs to reach out to these men with a tough message from God, no 'telly tubby' love theology will save these messed up masculines. Priests need to educate today's men and help them become responsible leaders.

What is needed today is a bit of strong male leadership to steer the church to full health. Not to capitulate to ideological demands. You're championing a popular idea, Fr Brian, but that does not mean God approves of it.

I do hope you have a change of heart.

I appreciate the challenge and thank you for your letter.

When we discuss some of the central issues facing us in the church, we will have to deal with opinions, positions and prejudices in a mature, positive way. It will not be easy. We need to learn to live with uncertainty in a healthy way. We need the guidance of the Holy Spirit. We need healing.

The Nuns (I)

For no reason at all, the following letter arrived in the postbag.
The simplicity of the letter made it very effective. It said:

> I know there are a lot of sad stories out there about the church
> and about nuns. I want you to know there are good nuns as
> well. I was a child in the convent in Cobh for the first eight and
> a half years of my life. The Mercy nuns were there. I can say,
> hand on my heart, that I loved it. I don't remember any bad
> going on there. We got a slap if we were bold, but we were
> never beaten around.
>
> When I left there at eight and a half, my life then became
> hell. I am now 59 years old and still wish I had been left with
> the nuns. The nuns in that Mercy Covent were good and kind.
> To this day I still remember two or three of their names. Thank
> you for reading this.

And that comes from a person we will call FH Dublin, even
though she did give her full name and address.

As I say, it is a simple letter. But it was good to receive it.

The Nuns (II)

Irish nuns are not the only women religious who are barely surviving these hard times. Nuns are under attack and in some cases it is bishops who are leading the attack.

The Ryan Report has cast a pall over almost every convent and every nun in the country. And rightly so. Everyone agrees that the nuns who treated the vulnerable so cruelly in Industrial Schools and in Magdalene Laundries deserve the distain in which they are now held.

Those who allowed these malfunctioning women to continue to damage children, cannot complain about being in the dock either.

However, most reasonable people will also remember that many women religious, in Ireland and across the world, have in latter years stood firmly against social injustice and against the oppressive clerical culture which ruled them up until the 1990s.

Here and elsewhere, women religious have been standing up for feminism in a powerful way, even though some clergy still try to bully them back into submission.

Women religious have been brave in accepting the changes of the Second Vatican Council. Nuns as we knew them may be a dying breed, but they are not going down without a fight. They are choosing to live fully until they die and that's more than can be said for the vast majority of us priests or bishops.

In America, the nuns, because they have been so pro-active, are now the subject of a Roman Inquisition. For the next two years, women religious in America will endure what is euphemistically called Visitation from Rome. The point of it all is to round up the sisters and put them back in convents where they can be more easily controlled.

The nuns in America have wisely accepted the visitation with open arms. They say we have a story to tell and will be glad to tell it if you'll listen to us. As a writer in the *National Catholic Reporter* wrote recently: 'First the nuns should bring the Vatican visitors to their graveyards. There they'll see a story of how women religious were sent by their European convents and worked on the frontiers of an emerging America.'

'The thousands of sisters they sent like labourers to the harvest helped build the church in America, staffing schools, hospitals, orphanages; starting ministries wherever need presented itself, in the cities teaming with new immigrants, and the frontiers where sisters arrived hauling harps and pianos to educate the daughters of farmers; or unto the battlefields of the Civil War, nursing the wounded on both sides; or through earthquake and plague in California, to earn a place of respect in an otherwise hostile anti-Catholic America.'

The NCR went on to point out that in the sixties the sisters pushed the boundaries of Religious Life in a way that men never really did. They got themselves educated for the modern world in a way that most of the priests were too smug to do. They took a lead in civil rights and peace movements. They took up prison ministries, and they went to the developing world to educate and help many emerging countries. They wrestled with their vocations and found new ways to help society.

Today there are almost 60,000 women religious in America, many of them aging but still active.

What causes most ripples in Rome is the fact that the women took the Second Vatican Council seriously. They left behind what needed to be left behind and they claimed their own vocations, lives and futures. In other words, they crept out from under the control of the bishops. Rome doesn't like it.

In America and here, one can't help but wonder if the new found conscience which some bishops have discovered overnight, is not another attempt to remind the women religious of their proper place in a male-dominated institution.

The vast majority of women religious in Ireland today will be the first to ensure that reparation will be made for the sins of their mothers. You can count on real nuns to speak and act justly.

The nuns will embrace powerlessness much more humbly than the clerics will. My only fear is that age will drive them into silence. I hope that never happens because the voice of gifted, holy women, from the time of Sarah to this present day, was the best expression of the authentic voice of a compassionate God.

Money matters in church

In a parish in New York the following note was slipped into the Sunday morning collection basket:

> Dear Pastor, in response to your recent letter about church support, I wish to inform you that the present condition of my bank account makes it almost impossible for this middle-age man to be of much help. My shattered financial condition is due to the Federal Laws, State Laws, County Laws, corporation laws, mother-in-laws, sister-in-laws, and outlaws. Through these laws I am compelled to pay a business tax, amusement tax, a head tax, a school tax, a gas tax, a light tax, a water tax, and a sales tax.
>
> I'm also expected to contribute to every organisation or society which the genius of man is capable of bringing into life. I carry life insurance, property insurance, medical insurance, liability insurance, burglary insurance, accident insurance, business insurance, earthquake insurance, tornado insurance, flood insurance, unemployment insurance, old age insurance and fire insurance.
>
> I have been inspected, expected, disrespected, rejected, dejected, examined and re-examined, informed and reformed, summoned, fined and compelled – until I provide an inexhaustible supply of money for every known need, desire or hope of the human race.
>
> I can tell you honestly that had not the unexpected happened, I could not have sent this cheque. The wolf that came to my door has just had pups in my kitchen. I sold them so here's the money.

Thankfully I never received a note like that in my collection basket – there are hardly any notes of any kind in it! Which reminds me of the English Vicar I met recently.

I was sharing a wedding in England in a beautiful Anglican church out in the country. It was small, ancient, whitewashed and idyllic. There were a goodly number of guests present. I was assisting the Vicar, a very proper lady with her hair pulled tightly back in a ponytail, and dressed in serious clerical gear. She did the ceremony in a detached, awfully correct manner, proper but without much personality.

At the end she had a list of people to thank. Then she added, 'We do not hold collections during marriage services in this church. However, you may like to contribute something to the up-keep of our little church and if you do so, we will be most grateful. To facilitate your gift giving I have placed a basket at each exit door. If you wish to place a donation in it, we will accept it grate-fully.

'If you prefer not to make a donation, we understand fully. However if you are making a donation, we have found, over the years, that it is a great help if you can fold it before you put it in the basket.'

We realised it was an effective, ingenious and not so subtle way to remind us to give generously. I wish I had thought of it first. It worked too.

There it is again – the women will save the church!

Prayer does not come easy

If we are to heal our wounded church, prayer will be at the heart of it. Sadly we rarely hear any talk of prayer now in churches. Prayer does not come easily to me, but what is becoming increasingly real is a spirit of gratefulness. I'm not the only one.

There's an elderly Benedictine monk who lives in America called David Steinel-Rast who says that the beginning of all prayer is gratefulness. 'The starting point for grateful living is the understanding that everything is given to us for free, as a gift, starting with life itself. So if we approach our lives that way, feeling like we are open for the surprise of what comes next, then we remain hopeful we can improve our lives', he says.

Gratefulness begins with being open to surprises. You may not even feel that you can be grateful, or you may feel that you are inadequately grateful. Just stop and be surprised. Everybody can do that.

'Before you open your eyes in the morning you can stop and be surprised that you have eyes to open, because there are more than 40 million people in the world who do not have eyes or cannot see with them. You can go through your day and, moment by moment, be surprised about anything and everything,' he says.

'This is the beginning of being grateful because the next consideration is "How come I have this? How come this is given to me?" Once you become conscious that something's given to you and you didn't earn it, buy it or achieve it, then you recognise you have to be grateful for it. When you realise that everything is given to you, then you are already on the road to giving thanks.'

He suggests we should have an image of a small vessel filling up. If we keep the vessel small, it will always be overflowing. That means we will have enough and not want more. The problem with the modern world, he contends, is that we want more and more and are never satisfied. The little vessel becomes a huge tank which can never be filled. It means that we are never really grateful.

'The affluent society makes the vessel bigger and bigger and that is why we find that the poor people everywhere are much more grateful than the rich, who expect to have everything.'

He says the secret is to make our vessels smaller. 'We can do that by living frugally and by continually asking what we really need and by distinguishing our *needs* from our *wants* … It is very important to do this because, in the world in which we live, we cannot just go on taking more than our own share.'

There is no secret to a contented way of life. Start by being grateful. Make your mind up to live gratefully. Very soon it will become more than a feeling – it will become an attitude towards life. The moment you have an attitude of gratefulness, you will be happy.

The monk is absolutely right. If you want to find more about his way of life look up www.gratefulness.org.

Here are some quotes about gratefulness which might help to start you on the road to appreciate the good things in your life:

- Give thanks for a little and you will find a lot. *Nigerian proverb*
- A thankful person is thankful under all circumstances. A complaining soul complains even in paradise. *Baha'i Faith*
- Gratitude for the gift of life is the primary wellspring of all religions. The hallmark of the mystic and the source of all true art … it is a privilege to be alive in this time when we can choose to take part in the self-healing of our world. *Joanna Macy, Buddhist*
- Gratitude is the most exquisite form of courtesy. *Jacques Maritain*
- Sanctity has to do with gratitude. To be a saint is to be fuelled by gratitude, nothing more and nothing less. *Ronald Rolheiser*

Green Shoots of Christian living

I don't know what it is, but people want to talk about religion more than they used to. When I explain to people that clerical power won't be a problem ten years from now because there will be so few clerics left, they seem surprised. Most religious orders, men and women, are struggling; in ten years they'll be reduced to a few communities each. Parish clergy will be centred in main towns only.

Even those who don't go to church are shocked to see the rapid demise of the Catholic Church's structures in Ireland.

The fact that we have been predicting it for twenty years has not made it easier to accept.

It surprises me that those who have no allegiance to religion are so saddened that the male celibate priesthood can no longer keep the show on the road.

Of course, there are people who are ecstatic at the demise of the Catholic Church which they have experienced as oppressive and destructive.

A growing number, though, recognise that we need to reflect deeply about the future.

I was speaking to a middle-aged man recently. He was distraught because his children never darken the door of a church. All of them got married in church but, as far as he knows, they haven't been there since. He and his wife did everything they could to hand on the faith. They gave them a good education in Catholic schools. They passed on moral values. Yet he knows his grandchildren will be told nothing about God, religion, prayers, or what it means to live in a Christian community.

He was looking for advice. I had none to give. He knew it was pointless arguing that they should go to Mass because the Catholic Church says so; or because it's a sin if they don't. He tried to tell them they will regret it later. In fact, though, they seem to be doing fine without any formal religion in their lives.

They are good people. They work hard. They make sacrifices for their children. They have a sense of justice and a sense of human morality. In times of trouble they believe in a God of sorts.

But there is nothing of substance to hand on. There is nothing beyond this world. There is no vision.

It has become fashionable not to go to church. You'd think, by reading about the 'In People' that nobody attends church now. The hard fact is that, while people don't attend church in the same numbers as before, there are a still huge numbers attending. They go because they want to and because they have searched around until they found a service which in some real way speaks of the world they experience.

As we priests become older, the problem will escalate. I was talking to parents recently who made a huge effort to bring their children to Mass. When they got there, the priest was cantankerous, in bad humour and scolded his way through the service. The parents and children agreed they would have been better to stay at home. And so they would.

And yet if we are to find a better way to live, to make the world a safer place, to have principles which help us with the changing issues of the day, we cannot do it alone. We need a believing community which helps to sustain us and guide us. Unless our search for the common good is supported by a community, it will perish sooner rather than later.

Being part of a Christian Community which is truly alive is infinitely more hopeful than making heroic journeys on our own.

Many who have given up on religion still believe in a benign God and still have a sense of the spiritual. They have no time for organised religion. I understand the point they are making, but I'm convinced we need a community to be part of, and sometimes to fight with. We need support and we need a safe, though challenging, place to grow. We need structures; we might not need the ones we have, but we do need some common bond, some sense of tradition, to see us through.

Even though I am critical of so much of organised religion, and the Catholic Church in particular, I still believe in the beauty of faith, in prayer, rituals for the significant moments of our lives, a sense of the sacred, a place of compassion, love and forgiveness. I would find it impossible to live without the hope that a truly

Christian community brings. I would be lost without the support of people to journey with and to pray with.

I was in the confessional room one afternoon recently looking after the daily duty in our monastery at the Graan.

A man whose marriage was in difficulty because of his drug abuse came in for a chat. He wasn't sure why he came. He had no idea what he wanted to hear, but he appreciated a safe place to talk. We didn't solve many problems, but he went out convinced that he had found a way to begin the healing journey again.

Shortly afterwards an elderly man came shuffling in. He began with these words: 'It's 55 years since my last confession.' I tried to not look as shocked as I was. I listened as he went through a life which was a mixture of sinfulness, failure, struggling, virtue and eventually a sense of hope. I asked why he came today. 'Because after a lifetime of running in every direction, I now realise that the church I was born into is the only place I can find the forgiveness I need,' he answered.

Despite the faults and failings of the human institution; despite the sinfulness of us priests, despite the anger that seeps through the lives of so many, there is something beautiful and graced-filled about a Christian Community which, not only promises forgiveness, but welcomes home the Prodigal Son with a hug and a party.

The awful clerical, power-hungry church is dead. The green shoots of Christian living are sprouting.

Who would want to be a priest?

If the sermon is long: 'He sends us to sleep.'
If it's short: 'He didn't bother to prepare it.'
If he raises his voice: 'He's shouting.'
If he speaks normally: 'You can't hear him.'
If he's away: 'He's always on the road.'
If he's at home: 'He never goes anywhere.'
If he's out visiting: 'He's never at home.'
If he's in the house: 'He never visits the people.'
If he talks finance: 'He's fond of money.'
If he doesn't: 'He's letting the parish run down.'
If he takes his time: 'He'd wear you out.'
If he doesn't: 'He never listens.'
If he starts Mass on time: 'His watch must be fast.'
If he starts a minute late: 'He holds everyone up.'
If he's young: 'He has no experience.'
If he's old: 'He ought to retire.'
And if he dies, or is changed:
'No one could ever replace him!'

Loving and Living

If you want to make God laugh tell him your plans. That was a thought which came to my mind as I went out for my early morning meditation / walk. April is time when nature is barely awakening from its winter slumber. As I walked along the country roads and saw signs of buds and flowerings, it was easy to know that God is rising to new life in nature. The words of Patrick Kavanagh came to mind:

Oh give me faith
that I may be
alive when April ecstasy
dances in every whitethorn tree.

There were thorn blossoms in bloom but I am reliably told they were the white blossoms of blackthorns. The birds were chirping and I stopped to listen as God spoke to me in the silence of the countryside, in the new clothes that nature was putting on hedges and ditches, in petals dropping off the trees almost like snow and in shy primroses making the grass look green again after its winter scorching.

My favourite oak tree seems to be enjoying its own resurrection. It was easy to pray: 'O give me faith, that I maybe alive when April's ecstasy dances in every whitethorn tree.'

As I walked I began to question myself gently. Am I really alive? Have I left the past behind? Am I willing to risk and trust so that I can have a future? Am I willing to believe that God is still walking with me? Have I any life left within me?

Many of us who are professional religious people choose to stay in the past and be comfortable, rather than risk a future for ourselves. Most of us in fact are more comfortable choosing death than we are choosing life. Yet the gospel stories after the resurrection ask the most important question of all: 'Why look for the living among the dead?'

Whatever about the desperate failings of the clerical institutional church, it's time for the rest of us to move to new places and to join the real world. It's time to accept the challenge, to make

God real to the present world in a way that is gentle and saving. It may mean leaving buildings, places and structures behind. But our mission is not about any of those things – it's about a message of hope for those who need it; a message of peace for the troubled; a message of life for those who flounder under the deaths of outdated structures.

When I came in to say Mass, the gospel summed it up. The disciples, who had betrayed and denied Jesus, were asked one simple question: 'Do you love me?' It wasn't about confession or repentance or humiliation. Love conquerors everything, including sin.

Our God is more interested in our future prospects than in our past failures. Our God is disgusted by abuse and those who covered up. But our God is greater than the puny efforts of clerical clubs and criminals and sinners.

I stepped in the refreshing shower and, as I was shaving, I told myself, 'If I can still love I am still alive.'

The Vatican – the facts

Some facts about Vatican City which seems to be in the news for a lot of reasons, mostly bad: Vatican City is an independent State. It is the only all-male State in the world. It has a population of 921 (approx) headed by Pope Benedict XVI. The Vatican is also the world's smallest State. And the fact that it has an all male population makes me wonder how they achieve even the reported 0.01% population growth each year.

It has no coastline, no natural resource; its main religion is Roman Catholicism. The prominent ethnic groups are Italians and Swiss, with Italian and Latin being its main languages. Its government style is ecclesiastical, which is another word for dictatorship.

The population of the State quadruples ever morning with the arrival of 3,000 lay people who work there.

Vatican Council II

You can tell what's important to a group by what they celebrate. Recently the GAA celebrated right royally the fact that they were founded 125 years ago. It's not usual to celebrate a 125th anniversary. And it's certainly not usual to do it with such extravagance. But they are proud of themselves and their organisation. And they have every right to be. So, well done for celebrating it in such an unapologetic way.

You'd think that the Golden Jubilee of one of the greatest moments in the church's history would be celebrated enthusiastically too. But there was hardly a word about the convocation of the Second Vatican Council. On 25 January 1959 in the Basilica of St Paul Outside the Walls in Rome, a grand old Pope, John XXIII, announced his intention to convoke what was known as an Ecumenical Council. It was followed by three and half years of preparation and, on 11 October 1962 Vatican II, as it became known, opened.

Poor old Pope John didn't live to see its fruition and more's the pity. He died on 3 June 1963 after only one of the four sessions had been completed.

John announced the council against stern opposition. For 19 years Pius XII had ruled with an iron fist and anyone who suggested new changes in theology was dealt with in much the same way as they are now. John XXIII, however, saw that it was an injustice and that the church did need to be reformed radically before it could dialogue honestly with the world.

The old Pope kept diaries which became famous after his death. He noted in the diary for 25 January 1959 that the assembled cardinals had greeted his announcement of the forth-coming council with 'Impressive devout silence'. It was partly surprise but mainly it was disapproval. So it's little wonder then that the church today had the same 'impressive devout silence' about the Golden Jubilee of Pope John's wonderful announcement.

John himself had been a stop-gap Pope. He was elected in October 1958 close to his 77th birthday. They knew he was in failing health and that he wouldn't last long, but it would give them breathing space to elect a *real* Pope.

John XXIII had a different idea. He knew he had a short time to live so he wanted to follow through on what the Holy Spirit wanted him to do. His decision to call the council was his alone because he would have been blocked if he had shared with others. He explained: 'It was motivated solely by concern for the good of souls and in order that the new Pontificate may come to grips, in a clear well-defined way with the spiritual needs of the present time.' The idea for the council had come to him as a flash of inspiration from heaven.

He asked the cardinals across the world to send him some helpful suggestions. Even though he wrote to each of them personally, only a small percentage replied and the majority of those who did, made it clear they disapproved.

John issued a new and cordial invitation: 'To the faithful of the separated churches to participate with us in this feast of grace.' But when the Pope's words were published, they had been changed by those close to him without his knowledge. The non-Catholic churches were down-graded to mere 'communities'.

Despite the opposition, miraculous changes did occur at the Second Vatican Council. Sadly, for the last 30 years or so there has been a dedicated effort to row back on those changes. And if you need a reason as to why the church is struggling for credibility in the world today, it is because of that rejection of grace from the Holy Spirit.

However, be assured that all the opposition in the world will not stifle the Holy Spirit. And the old institutions and the dinosaurs who have blocked God's spirit will all disappear in time. A merciful beautiful church that we can all be proud of will emerge from the rubble.

I can be certain of that, because it is inevitable when mere human beings take on the role of being God they always end in failure. From the story of Adam and Eve to the present day, that's how it has been. God never loses patience. God never loses.

Picking a Cardinal

I got this very insightful letter from a man living in Roscommon. He had read the piece I wrote about the kind of qualities people were looking for in whoever should be the next Archbishop of Westminster in England.

> On reading your article in the *Sunday World*, 'Cardinal Will Be A Hard Act To Follow,' I totally agree with what you said. If Jesus applied for the job he wouldn't stand a chance of getting it.
>
> Now I am an uneducated man but have 76 years of living behind me and that has taught me a thing or two. Having being brought up on a wee farm in Cavan and worked that farm for over 50 years, I now look back and think about life then. Our old folks worked very hard and for long hours, plus the fact they were half starved.
>
> In church on Sunday, it was common to see people fainting and having to be carried out to the fresh air to recover. Such good people have all passed on, and some lie in unmarked graves. In my mind they are unsung saints. Did anyone approach any of them to offer them a position as a bishop or cardinal? Not in a million years. Saints are never on the agenda for that office.
>
> Perhaps you are now thinking to yourself, 'What the hell has the past got to do with the future?' Well it has a lot to do with it. Who did Christ pick for his twelve bishops?
>
> My choice of Cardinal would be a good living man, living in an ordinary house, doing an honest day's work for an honest day's pay and supporting his wife and family. There's no closer than that to living the gospel.
>
> Yours truly, Roscommon Man.

Now isn't he a sensible man?

But, Father, what do you actually do?

Written by a parish priest who has since – perhaps understandably! – retired.

Leader of people, wisest of guides;
   diplomat, elder, who never takes sides.
Inspirer, Confessor, forgiver of sins;
   caretaker, cleaner and emptier of bins.
Welcome baptiser of infants in arms;
   counter of candles and filler of forms.
Father and teacher, chaplain to schools;
   chairman of governors, maker of rules.
Parish accountant and administrator;
   typist and banker, and news duplicator.
Signer of Mass cards, reference composer,
   certificate writer and passport endorser.
Digger of gardens, inspector of drains,
   checker of roofs every time that it rains.
Redesigner of churches, to fill empty pews,
   reglazer of windows, repairer of loos.
Visitor, caller, knocker on doors,
   target of gossips and cadgers and bores.
Chaplain to hospital, long or short stay,
   'Please don't forget, my Mum's in for the day.'
The doctors and nurses all merit a call,
   smile kindly at everyone – keep on the ball!
Sayer of Masses and liturgy leader,
   celebrant, sacristan, cantor and reader.
Marshall of servers, collectors and choir;
   of hymn books and papers – both seller and buyer.
President of Eucharist, calm as you like –
   'but did I remember to switch on the mike?'
Celebrant of Masses, devotions and prayers,
   patient receiver of everyone's cares.
Marriage encounter and parish renewal;
   Journeys of Faith and liturgical jewels.

Shepherd to prayer groups, prophet and pastor;
    spiritual director and guru and master.
Help of the sick and anointer and healer;
    support for the dying and final appealer.
Conductor of funerals, comfort of mourners,
    called to give solace to even the scorners.
Minister of marriage, the guide of young love,
    adviser of couples who need help from above.
Provider of insight into all life connubial;
    collector of forms for marriage tribunal.
Man of prayer and reflection, of study and thought,
    but still finding time for the news and the sport.
Something for everyone, you might exclaim,
    but when things go wrong who is it they blame?

(Courtesy of Pastoral Renewal Exchange)

PART FOUR

Healing our wounded world

Changes in Church and Society

In the thirty plus years that I have been writing for the *Sunday World* I have chronicled a vast quantity of events, voiced an embarrassing number of opinions, and noticed changes in society which could not have been foreseen when I began writing here.

It's this latter point which confuses me. More and more I have begun to write less and less about what happened and think more and more about *why* it happened.

For example, in that time I have seen the disappearance of almost every structure within the Catholic Church.

When I began writing for the *Sunday World* in the mid 70s I was six years ordained and had been editor of a magazine for five years. I was working in the Catholic Communications Institute. By night I was chaplain to the ballrooms of Dublin. Everywhere I went I dressed in black with a white clerical collar because it would have been regarded as a serious fault not to, and some vague edict of the Maynooth statutes insisted that I had to.

I lived in a Monastery which had over 80 monks praying, and working at God knows what. There were plenty of students and if you stepped out of line as a student, you were promptly sent home because there were others to take your place.

I am quite aware I am writing about a world most of you never knew existed, and I might as well be writing about events three hundred years rather than thirty years ago. It is impossible for the modern day reader to imagine what it was like then.

But in the 70s we were convinced the society we lived in would never change and would never end. As it happened, everything collapsed, not quite overnight, but not far from it.

Back then I did more than my fair share of weddings. In one year, I did 181 weddings. I ate turkey and ham at 180 of those – one had lamb. None of the couples admitted to living together before their marriage. Few if any had a child before they were married and passports were so controlled that the girl's name was sent to the passport office and a new passport in her married name was issued. It was sent to the priest and he could not hand it over until she was married and had taken on her new name.

I could go on but it would depress me.

I think by now you get the point that the world has changed. If I'm really honest I'll admit that I am far more at home in the world of today than I was in that world of the 70s. I was never comfortable being part of a society where big business, money and powerful institutions bullied the individual. Make no mistake, that is precisely what they did.

But perhaps the biggest change of all has come in family life. How, for example, would you define a family today?

I notice that the same problem is occupying the pages of the British press these days. Why are so many young people dying from guns, knives and violent behaviour? Why are so many young people taking their own lives? Why do people continue to take drugs knowing that it will destroy them? Why do they not care?

Clifford Longley, writing in the *Tablet*, shared his views. As well as being a writer and thinker, he is also a Youth Magistrate in England. He said that we should not give more powers to governments and police, but should think about ways to close the gap between generations. One of the reasons large sections of the younger generation are virtually uncontrollable is the breakdown in family life, he says. It is not a one-parent versus two-parent issue nor is it poverty related.

> One sees every day a lack of nerve on the part of parents who are no longer sure they have the right to impose restrictions on their children's freedom. They do not know how to say no, nor how to socialise their children to fit into an orderly society. The passing down of the secrets of good parenting seems to have come to a halt.

It is so deep rooted that the very basic values and beliefs of society have to be questioned and changed.

He had some interesting facts too. British teenagers spend less time with parents than any other teenagers in Europe. They have less respect for their parents and are among the least happy young people in the world. Furthermore, they abuse sex, alcohol and drugs earlier than any other European country and inevitably they are the most violent too.

I wonder are the same trends obvious here in Ireland? I would suggest in many urban areas at least, we are running a close second to Britain.

When family life breaks down there is nowhere to go. No state, no police authority, no pious platitudes in the media, can replace it.

Sadly it's probably too late for the present crop of teenagers but could we, as a society, begin to agree on what a family *is* and could we begin to support family life above everything else?

The future generations might then have some framework and values handed down to them. We will not solve the problem by denying that it exists.

So what if Religious Orders pass away? So what if church structures pass away? So what if society changes beyond recognition? All those are part of the natural process of things. But when the basic unit of society collapses, that's a disaster.

Facts about Hunger

Hunger is the number one health risk in the world. So we should learn the facts:

1. Over 1 billion people go to bed hungry every night.
2. The highest proportion of undernourished people in the world reside in Africa.
3. Five million children die of hunger or hunger related diseases every year.
4. When it comes to the chronically hungry, women suffer more than men. 60% of the chronically hungry people in the world are women.
5. Every six seconds a child dies of hunger somewhere in the world.
6. In developing countries it is estimated that over 146 million people are under weight.
7. 60% of deaths worldwide are caused by malnutrition and other hunger related diseases.
8. Finally the biggest scandal of all is that in a world where 1 billion people go to bed hungry every night, it is also a fact that 1 billion people in the world suffer from obesity.

Who can you trust?

The American theologian John Shea has a simple story about trust. He tells of a man who spent his youth searching for meaning.

One day he was lucky to meet God as he journeyed on the road. He took the opportunity to seek his help: 'God, how can I find happiness?'

God said, 'I have been travelling all day. Could you please get me a drink of water?'

So the man went into a village to get the drink of water for God. In the village he knocked on a door and a beautiful girl welcomed him. He asked her for a drink of water for God.

She said, 'Maybe you need one yourself, so come in.' He did. It was midday so they shared a beautiful lunch too. After that he couldn't leave. So he married the girl raised a family and stayed for 30 years. He had a really meaningful life.

One day, after 30 years, he was out walking when a ferocious storm blew up. He cried out, 'God please save me,' and God said, 'What about the drink of water?'

You can take many meanings out of that but one of them is that when life is going great we forget God. We seem to call on God only when we're in trouble. But God reminds us that relationship is a two way street. Don't turn your back on me just because you don't need me. Keep in touch in good times if you wish to recognise me in bad times.

Which prompts a few more questions: Where is God in my life? How important is it for me to have a God I can trust? Have I still a childish rather than a childlike relationship with God? And what happens when everything I trusted in collapses?

Albert Einstein once said, 'Only a life lived for others is worth living.' John Wesley, one of the founding brothers of the Methodist Movement, said much the same: 'Do all the good you can, by all the means you can, in all the ways you can, at all the times you can, to all the people you can, as long as ever you can.'

But I like St Augustine's motto best: 'Love God and do what you like!'

Broadcasting

Change is never easy. For over 20 years I have been a contributor to *Pause for Thought* on BBC Radio 2. It's on air at a quarter past nine every morning and, since sixteen of those years was in the company of Sir Terry Wogan, the audience was massive. Sometimes it reached out to over 8 million listeners.

Terry was the easiest man in the world to work with, forever encouraging. At 71 he deserves his rest.

He has been succeeded by Chris Evans. The *Pause for Thought* team all wondered if we'd get the sack. But Chris said he wanted us to be part of his programme too. A select group, representing various major religions, was chosen as we set about fitting into the new format. My first four weeks on *Pause for Thought* with Chris was a really challenging experience. Chris is just as interested as Terry was in what you have to say, but wants a different kind of delivery. You have to be able to chat to the man face to face. It's different. It's challenging. And it is most rewarding. We now have nine million listeners

The BBC has many faults and as a corporation makes many mistakes. However, as somebody who has worked with them for well over 20 years now, they take religion seriously. If you broadcast in an interesting way, write scripts that are appealing, and turn up on time to do the job, the BBC appreciates a professional. It doesn't matter what your point of view is, they will treat you with fairness and respect as a broadcaster. Not every station I've broadcast with was as impartial.

I spend a lot of time working for them now; I am delighted to get a voice in the marketplace.

The BBC takes religion seriously because it spends money on it. It doesn't work on the cheap like many of the organisations I have been associated with before.

Every Sunday night I host a programme called *Sunday Half Hour* on BBC Radio 2. It has a huge audience and has been going for 70 years. I am the first Catholic priest to host it. I was reluctant to accept it because I thought I was not suitable for the programme. But the BBC insisted I was.

I have been doing it for three years. Within the half hour there are 8 hymns, scripture quotations, reflections, blessings and prayers.

The choirs are specifically recorded by the BBC from all over Britain and Ireland. The hundreds of thousands who tune in each Sunday evening are at the upper end of the age scale. For many of them it's their only opportunity to be part of a service on Sunday. Many of them reside in homes or are part of parishes which no longer hold services. Others are travelling back to their work and look forward to the half hour which puts them in touch with their inner spirit.

The listeners insist that I give a blessing at the end of the programme because they say it's the only chance they have to receive a blessing. Most of them have their hymn books out well in advance so that they can sing along with the choir. You might say it's *Songs of Praise* on the radio. Except that it was going 40 years before *Songs of Praise* was heard of.

For our listeners it is a sacred space which they enjoy. The BBC goes to great expense to provide them with that sacred space on the most popular radio channel they have.

Pause for Thought is the same. They accept good broadcasters, some of whom are clergy, from all of the main faiths, and give them a real chance to communicate with the masses. It is supposed to last two minutes but with both Terry and Chris it is usually between 4 and 5. I always feel I am part of the programme and not an imposition. It's a real attempt to give people a positive thought which carries them through the day. It's not a token, meaningless, spot squeezed in at the least important parts of the day out of a sense of duty.

On other stations I worked with, especially RTÉ, religion seemed to be tolerated, at best.

Chris Evans is enthusiastic, full of energy a great listener and couldn't be more encouraging. He knows better than anyone that there is a market for relevant thoughts well packaged and well delivered.

In short, religion doesn't have to be about child abuse, wayward clerics, arguments about money and hand ringing, by people who want to run churches even though they never attend them.

We need debate, we need honesty, we need integrity, but we also need people of conviction. We need to be aware of a deep need within us for spirituality. We need to realise that there is more to broadcasting than creating controversy.

Surely after the Celtic Tiger's collapse, we should have learned the lesson.

A Shepherd

One day a shepherd was bringing his entire flock of sheep from one part of his farm to another. He was crossing the public highway when a large BMW pulled up beside him. The driver was a young man dressed in a Bruin suit, Gucci shoes, Ray-Ban glasses. He leaned out his window and said to the shepherd, 'If I tell you exactly how many sheep you have in your flock, will you give me one?'

The shepherd looked at the man, then looked at his large flock of sheep and answered calmly, 'Sure.'

The young over-weight businessman parked his car, took out his laptop, connected it to his I-phone, surfed the net, called up a GPB satellite navigation system, scanned the area, sent an email on his I-phone and after a few minutes received a response. Finally he printed out a 20 page report on his miniaturised printer and turned to the shepherd triumphantly with the result: 'You have 1493 sheep.'

'That is the right answer,' said the shepherd, 'And you can take one of the sheep.'

The young businessman got out of the car, took a good look at the flock, selected one of the animals and bundled it into his car.

Then the shepherd said to him, 'If I tell you exactly what your business is, will you give me back my animal?'

'That seems a fair bargain to me,' the young man answered.

'Clearly you're a consultant,' said the shepherd.

'That's the right answer,' replied the young man. 'But how did you know that?'

'It was easy,' said the shepherd, 'You turned up here uninvited. You want to get paid for an answer I already knew, to a question I never asked, and you know absolutely nothing about sheep. Now you can give me my collie dog back?'

Shepherds are wise people. As the Psalm says: 'The Lord is my shepherd, there is nothing I shall want ... he guides me along the right paths... he is true to his name.'

Faith in the World

Here's a question for you: Why do people believe in God? It's a difficult question to answer because there are many people who have faith, but don't believe in what we call God. For example, I have many friends in Alcoholics Anonymous. They believe in A Higher Power. Their higher power might not be the God of religion but they really do believe in a sustaining and effective power in their lives which is beyond rational explanation.

When it comes to God I like to keep things as simple as possible. I don't like delving into proofs of God's existence or exploring the tensions between science and religion. Too often that's a dialogue of the deaf.

However, there is one view expressed by Richard Dawkins which I agree with. He says that cathedrals, beautiful music, moving stories and parables do help people believe a bit. 'But,' he maintains, 'by far the most important variable, determining your religion, is an accident of birth.'

It's hard to disagree with that. The place where I was born, in Northern Ireland, the kind of parents I had, the school I went to, all helped to determine the faith I now have. Of course I was also free to accept or to reject that faith. I still struggle to keep on searching positively.

These days I question my faith and my beliefs often. That used to worry me. Not any longer. If the God I believe in is relevant, then it won't be a frightening God from my childhood memory. It will be a God who helps me find a peaceful, harmonious way through life's difficulties. My search for God never ends and, luckily, his search for me never ends either.

I can live peacefully with not having all the answers. I once believed that the opposite of faith is doubt. Now I know that the opposite of faith is not doubt but certainty. If we are certain about beliefs, where's the need for faith? The healthy scepticism which rules my life now has helped me to change, to grow and to be undisturbed in this ever changing world.

This prayer, which was found in the cell of a Jewish prison in Cologne, expresses it well:

I believe in the sun even when it is not shining.
I believe in love even when I cannot feel it.
I believe in God even when God is silent.

Prison

I have been ministering in prisons for years now and I suspect, rightly or wrongly, there are some people who believe that many prisoners are worthless; that they are in prison because they deserve to be; that people feel safer when prisoners are locked up – preferably with the key thrown away.

I have also been the victim of crime and I know how victims feel. Yet I'm more convinced than ever that locking people away in prisons is an expensive, ineffective and often futile way of punishing those who break the law. Of course there are people who are so dangerous that they have to be locked away. But most could be made pay for their crimes through probation, rehabilitation or the use of restorative justice.

Jesus made no secret of how he felt about prisoners. He didn't distinguish between the innocent and the guilty but said that when we minister to prisoners, we minister to him. (Mt 23:36) Maybe that was because Jesus himself was imprisoned, as was John the Baptist, St Peter and St Paul – who wrote a few letters from behind bars. Other famous prisoners were saint Maximilian Kolbe who when he was in a Nazi concentration camp, voluntarily accepted death so that the life of a fellow prisoner with a young family could be saved. The Lutheran theologian Dietrich Bonhoeffer famously resisted Hitler's philosophy of hate. He was imprisoned and put to death because of his convictions.

For some, at least, prisons were places of grace.

I believe that all humans are created by God and should be given the chance to change, repent and reform.

It's a major problem because there are close to 90,000 prisoners in Britain this morning and it costs £40,000 per year to keep each prisoner there. There are 150,000 children who have a parent in prison. Here's another disturbing fact. The suicide rate of men in prison is five times greater than in the outside community.

There must be a better way to help both prisoners and victims in this day and age!

Take your time

I love stories with a message. I believe that all stories are true; some of them actually happened. Which means the 'truth' within the story is more important than the details of it. That is why I love the story about the farmer who carried his pig to market.

As he struggled to walk with his lovely fat pig in his arms, he met a visitor from the town on the way. They stopped to chat. 'Why are you carrying the pig?' the visitor asked. 'Because I want him fresh and healthy when we get to the market', the farmer answered.

'Do you have only one pig to sell?'

'No, I have ten of them to sell,' the farmer said proudly. 'When I have this one sold, I'll walk back and carry another one to the market.'

'Would it not be easier to get a trailer and bring all ten in together?' ventured the visitor, 'Surely it would save time.'

The farmer looked puzzled. 'Sure, what difference does time make to a pig?' he said.

Maybe the farmer was right. Time doesn't matter much to a pig, but it's a mystery to us. Where does time go? How can I use time more fruitfully? Have I much time left? All good questions, but in the end, does it really matter that much?

It takes five years for the seed of a bamboo tree to show any growth above the ground, and then it shoots up often to a height of 90 feet in six weeks. In the five years of preparation, strong roots spread underground to access food and to give it stability. Then, and only then, does it take off. We on the other hand want instant results. But what is special and worthwhile always needs nurturing and patience.

'Time is too slow for those who wait, too long for those who grieve, too short for those who rejoice, but for those who love, time is eternal.'

Take time to enjoy the many lovely gifts around you. Each season is a beautiful season. Walk in the park, feast your eyes on the leaves, and look forward to cosy fires and restful evenings.

Make time to take little breaks throughout the day. Be patient with yourself and be patient with others.

Vincent Van Gogh was a troubled genius in many ways. But he once gave good advice. He said: 'The best way to know God is to love many things. Love a friend, love your husband, and love your wife. Love each day given to you. Take time to love and you will know God.'

I couldn't put it better myself.

The Fire Fighter

I was interested in a piece published recently in the *Boston Globe* newspaper. It reprinted a photograph which touched the heart of what then was a much divided city in 1968.

A fire destroyed a cluster of apartments in the suburb of Roxbury. One of the fire fighters was Bill Carroll. He crawled on his stomach through the thick smoke to find a little baby of Afro-American parents named Evangeline. He found the infant unconscious in her cradle and as he brought her from the apartment he tried to revive her by breathing life into her.

A newspaper photographer captured the image of a white fire fighter from the well off district of South Boston breathing life into a poor Afro-American baby at a time when racial tension was at its highest in America.

Carroll remained a fire fighter for another thirty-four years. Evangeline lost most of her family to drugs and illness but became a nursing and teaching assistant and raised a family of her own. She always wanted to meet the man in the photograph, the fire fighter who saved her life.

By now she had given up hope that it would ever happen. Then she read about another Boston fire fighter being killed in a crash while on his way to a fire. That made her think again. She said: 'I didn't want to leave this earth without saying thank you. If I did, my life would be incomplete.'

So with the help of the Boston newspaper she tracked down Bill Carroll. They met on the very site where he had saved her from certain death.

When they met he greeted her warmly: 'You have grown a lot since the last time I saw you! Thank you so much for remembering me.'

Evangeline admitted that without him she would not be alive. They hugged like long lost friends.

Evangeline feared that Carroll may have forgotten her. But she was reassured when he told her: 'Evangeline Harper, I will never forget her name if I live to be a 100 years old.' Delightfully their friendship continues and grows.

In tough days like these we need good news stories to keep our faith in goodness alive. By the way if you need to thank somebody who helped you, you should do it before it's too late.

Growing Up

When I was a child our family lived in a wee house out in the country. The kitchen was the centre of the house because it was where we worked, played, talked and had our meals. There was a flaming turf fire which provided all our heat and cooked all our food. We carried the turf from the bog beside us and when the fire was lit there was a cosiness, the thought of which comforts me to this day.

Then there was a big wooden table in the centre of the kitchen. We did everything around the table. We did our homework, played cards late at night, were in awe of our neighbours who dropped in and gossiped. And most of all it was where we ate our food.

Food was simple and home cooked. Plenty of homemade bread, and tea you could trot a mouse on. On special days we had a chicken cooked in a pot over the fire but mostly it was bacon and every kind of vegetable – straight from the garden outside. Especially the big flowery potatoes, or spuds as we called them, which my father had laboured over in the evenings after his real work.

But my lasting memory is that we all sat round the table to eat whether we liked it or not. There was no choice either when it came to helping prepare the food. My mother did most of it but we all had a hand in it. Afterwards all the dishes were put in a big basin, scalding water was poured over them and we took it in turns to dry them and put them away.

The point is that meals were religious rituals. We ate together every evening at the same time. We never started a meal without saying grace and we didn't finish one without showing gratitude. The big table in the centre of the kitchen wasn't just a feeding trough. It was an altar. We experienced love and togetherness. Sharing food made us a family.

I know times have changed and we don't have turf fires and not many big tables either. But family meals should still be sacred. In their own way they are as important as Eucharist in the church is. I think we should once again make food and not television the centre of homes. Share meals together, chat, listen, be human, be real. Being human is where we find each other and where we find God.

Life is difficult

I'm sure you've heard the story of the man who went on a fishing holiday to Scotland. He was a committed atheist, but that of course didn't make him a bad fisherman. He hired a boat and went far out into the deep lake and there he sat for hours enjoying the peace immensely.

Out of nowhere the Loch Ness monster popped out of the water and charged towards the boat. It seemed as if it could swallow the boat and the fisherman in one almighty gulp. The terrified atheist looked and pleaded: 'God, help me!' Just then a voice from heaven answered: 'I thought you didn't believe in me.' To which the atheist replied: 'Ah God, give me a break. Until a minute ago, I didn't believe in the Loch Ness Monster either.'

As we go through life our beliefs change. That's normal enough because life is a journey. On the journey our built-in Sat Nav is not always accurate and we can get lost. The good news is that getting lost is no bad thing. Because life is not just a journey, it's a search – a search for meaning, a search for fulfilment.

The Bible is littered with people who continue to journey and to search. They're pilgrims who get lost but who still find God. It's the same with us. Abram, for example, is told: 'Leave your country and your family … and I will bless you.'

Moses and Jonah eventually obeyed the same command. During the days of Lent we meet Jesus on long lonely journeys into the desert and up to the top of mountains. In the wilderness he meets himself and in the clouds he meets God – that's what getting lost does for you.

Robert Louis Stevenson once said: 'To travel hopefully is a better thing than to arrive, and the true success is to labour.' Most of us make the mistake of giving up too easily. We settle for a cosy existence.

Speaking of travelling, one of the most famous books of the latter part of the 20th century was Scott Peck's *The Road Less Travelled*. It was about making the difficult journey inwards to self-discovery. Perhaps one of the reasons for its success was the first line which said simply: 'Life is difficult.' Anyone who starts there is living in the real world.

Life is difficult but it is also beautiful. Try to survive the difficult and to really enjoy the beautiful.

A boy and his grandfather

There's a story I love about a boy and his grandfather. They decided to take their donkey to sell it in the marketplace. The wise old man walked slowly behind the donkey while his grandson walked beside the donkey's head holding on to the winkers. As they made their way down the road the neighbours began to laugh at them. They were so stupid to walk beside the donkey. Why not ride the animal?

So the grandfather, not wanting to be held to ridicule, put the young boy on the donkey's back. The neighbours now began to point their fingers accusingly at the young man. They said it was typical of the modern generation. He was selfish. He rode on the donkey's back and he let the poor old grandfather walk all the way to the market.

So the grandfather and the boy decided to change things around. After all they didn't want their neighbours to make fun of them.

This time the grandfather got up on the donkey's back and the young man walked beside the donkey. But once again the neighbours criticised the grandfather. How could he be so cruel as to make the young boy walk, by taking the easy way out and riding on the donkey's back himself?

There was nothing for it. The only way to satisfy the neighbours was for both of them to get on the donkey's back. This time the neighbours got in touch with the Society for the Prevention of Cruelty to animals. 'These two people were far too burdensome for the poor little donkey,' they said.

Eventually the old man and the boy came to the conclusion that the only thing they could do was to carry the donkey themselves. They tied the donkey's feet to a pole and hoisted the pole up on their shoulders with the donkey dangling between them. It was a mighty struggle for them and as they wearily crossed a bridge, all three of them fell into the river and had to be rescued.

The moral of the story is obvious enough. If you live your life solely to please others, you'll have a very unhappy life. No matter what you do you'll be wrong in someone's eyes. You can't please them all, so first please yourself.

Being surrounded by negative people drains us. We have to learn to choose what is right and do it, no matter what they think. As some sailing people put it so well, pessimists complain about the wind, optimists hope it will change; realists simply adjust the sails.

The Pace of life

Recently I was reading a piece in *The New York Times* by their columnist Thomas Friedman. He told a story about arriving at Charles de Gaulle airport in Paris to work for his column. He knew that a taxi would meet him. As he was coming out of the airport he saw his driver holding a board with his name written on it. He followed him.

The taxi man didn't speak but turned and walked towards the car, all the while speaking on a Bluetooth phone. Friedman got into the back of the car and handed the man a piece of paper with his destination written on it. As they went into the heavy traffic on the way into Paris, Friedman noticed that the driver of the car not only continued to talk on his Bluetooth, but actually switched on a video which was shown on a screen on the dashboard. He did all this as he was driving through the insane traffic in Paris.

It was getting on Friedman's nerves so he decided to calm himself by listening to his IPod. Later to distract himself, he took out a laptop and began to write the article that I was now reading.

He concluded that between himself and the driver they were actively doing six different things. The driver was working as a taxi man, talking on a Bluetooth and watching a video. Friedman was travelling from the airport, listening to an IPod and writing an article. At the end of the journey, which took an hour, Friedman got out, tipped him, went into the hotel and realised that the only thing they hadn't done was actually to speak to each other. He concluded that modern technology divides us more than it unites us.

He quoted a researcher called Linda Stone who calls this over activity 'Continuous Partial Attention'. It's a disease of the internet era. We are everywhere except where we actually are physically.

You can see then that gospel values have no chance of being fulfilled in such a generation. We are 'To love God with *all* our heart, *all* our soul, *all* our mind. And our neighbours as ourselves.'

If we are to attempt being fully present to one another, we need to unplug from the worst aspects of our over active society and its Continuous Partial Attention. It could be lethal if we're not careful.

Keep your heart up

Times are tough and many people are getting it hard to make ends meet. One of the many letters I got this week came from a mother writing about her married daughter who had a major accident which left her confined to a wheelchair. She and her small children were re-housed to an upstairs flat which was impossible for her. It was also a deprived area. She found rats in the bedroom.

At the end of the letter the grandmother added: 'When you are poor with no money, the future's always in another place.' And who could argue with that?

Many of us though, willingly, condemn ourselves to the same hopeless future when we refuse to change or look at new ways of living. Hell has been described as an eternity locked into the present with no possibility of change. Yet, mostly, life has possibilities.

'Live each day as if it were your last and one day you'll be right,' is good advice. Part of the problem is that living for today is not easy in the modern world.

We can make plans for the future but God decides where we go. As the Bible says, 'You do not know when the Lord is coming but be ready for him when he does.'

Did you ever stop to think what you'd do if you were told the end of your life was near? It happens to people every day. And I don't know how I would react if I was told that news.

Cardinal Newman said, 'To grow is to change, and to be perfect is to change often.' He also said, 'To be holy is not so much doing this or not doing that … but it is a state of mind of living habitually in the light of a better world.'

No matter how tough life is now, it won't last forever – there is always hope.

Alzheimer's Disease

Because I spend so much time in hospitals and nursing homes, one of my great personal fears is that I'll develop some form of Alzheimers. If it happens, there's not much I can do about it – but in the meantime I pray...

If a member of your family has dementia you'll understand some of the pain involved.

Rabbi Harold Kushner, in his book called *Overcoming Life's Disappointments*, writes about a man who devotes himself to his dying wife.

He had the same routine for years. Every afternoon he sat with his wife in the nursing home. Because she was suffering from Alzheimer's disease, she slipped further and further away into the fog of dementia with each passing day.

Every day he would feed her lunch. He would sit with her and show her pictures of their children. He would tell her the latest family news, and other stories she would forget as soon as she heard them.

He would patiently remind her who he was; explain that they were married and had been for the past 52 years; that they had two daughters and a son and four beautiful grandchildren.

He would hold her hand as she drifted in and out of consciousness. Before leaving, he would kiss her and tell her how much he loved her – and she would never realise nor remember that he had ever been there.

His heartbroken friends would ask him: Why do you keep going when she doesn't even know who you are?

And he would always reply: I keep coming because I know who I am.

What a wonderful insight into love, commitment and self-awareness that simple story gives us!

As the author John Mc Gahern wrote in his book, *Among Women*, 'The best journeys in life are always among the familiar ... You can only love what you know.'

Teddy and the Boston surgeon

Once, in mid-America, there was a young boy who as a child was born without sight. After many tests they realised he would never be able to see. At six years old he began to learn to live as a sightless person.

Out of the blue, word came that there was a young specialist in Boston who was pioneering a new form of surgery which might be able to help him. The local community raised sufficient funds to have the boy sent for tests. The tests showed that the operation might work.

More money was collected and the day came for him to go to Boston for his operation. His parents packed his case but the boy wanted only one 'friend' to go with him. That was a teddy bear which he'd had for most of his life. By now it had one ear chewed off, the button was gone from one eye and out through his belly button came the stuffing from his insides. There was also a smell because Teddy could never be washed.

The parents were embarrassed and didn't want to bring Teddy but the boy insisted. No Teddy – no operation. So Teddy went.

In the hospital, it was only when he was under anaesthetic for the operation that they were able to take Teddy away.

When he came out of the operation his eyes were bandaged for a number of weeks. He still held on to Teddy. The great day came when all the bandages were gently unwrapped and his eyes adjusted to brightness. Miraculously he could see. He saw Teddy with the one ear hanging off, the eye gone and the belly button protruding. He saw the face of his mother for the first time and the rest of his family too.

After a couple of weeks he was ready to go home. The surgeon came in to say goodbye because by now they were friends. As the surgeon was leaving the young boy called him back. He wanted to thank him for all he had done, and as a token of appreciation he handed over his precious Teddy to the surgeon.

The surgeon's first instinct was to refuse. But he realised the boy really appreciated the powerful gift the surgeon had given him and he in turn wanted to give back to the surgeon the most precious gift he had, which was Teddy. So the surgeon wisely took the teddy bear. He then had a cabinet erected in the foyer of the hospital where he worked and placed Teddy in it. Underneath was a card which read, 'The highest fee I have ever received.' It's a lesson in how to give and how to receive graciously. There are some gifts money can't buy.

Compassion

A scripture reading over Easter brought an incident from 20 years ago back to mind. It was the day the Governor of a prison phoned me and asked me to do a special favour for him. It was in the mid 1980s and it was not unusual for me to get a request from the Governor of that particular prison. Usually it was about somebody who was in danger of taking their own life. On this occasion it was different.

He wanted me to bring a prisoner to a hospital across the city. The prisoner's dying wife, who was in her early 30s, requested to see her husband before she died. The Governor couldn't arrange it officially so he asked me to do it quietly and to make sure that the prisoner came back. He took no chances though because he handcuffed the man to me. You can imagine what it was like trying to get in and out of a car handcuffed? And that's not even thinking about driving.

On the way over, the prisoner told me his problems started with alcohol. As a teenager he progressed to drugs and through drug abuse he had contracted the AIDS virus. He had passed on the AIDS virus to his wife and now she was dying from an AIDS related illness because of him. They had young children who were being cared for by her family. These days she could have lived longer, but there was no such treatment back then.

When I got to the room in the hospital, the most awful thing happened. I realised that I was still handcuffed to him. I couldn't leave the room for what should have been a private, special moment when they would speak to each other for the last time on this earth. The details of what they said must remain forever confidential.

But I can say that she told him she forgave him for passing on the illness which was now killing her and that he should not use it as an excuse to go on drinking or abusing drugs.

He must get treatment and help, to rear the children now that she couldn't do so.

I brought him back to the prison and she died that evening. I was the co-celebrant at her funeral three days later.

I'll never forget the readings at Mass: 'The souls of the virtuous are in the hands of God, no torment shall ever touch them' from the Book of Wisdom and St Paul's wonderful reading which we used at Easter: 'If we have been united with him in a death like his, we shall certainly be united with him in a resurrection like his.' I didn't feel so utterly helpless after that.

Faith tells me that there is a happy ending because of the Easter story. And that happy ending is gifted to each of us, which is why Easter is such a joyous time.

God's listening ear

I stopped looking for God up in the sky a long time ago. Instead, I now look around me. Last week I met God's great listening ear in a supermarket pushing a trolley. Let me explain. This 'listening ear of God' was a 40 year old mother of two. She is a teacher by day and on two nights a week she doubles up as a very Good Samaritan. Samaritans, and other helplines, allow a person in crisis to talk about their problems freely, especially when they feel no one else will listen.

As a volunteer with the group, my teacher friend listens on the phone to people who are so distressed that they are no longer sure if they want to go on living. The distraught people who ring her must feel very lucky indeed when they hear her quiet, re-assuring compassionate voice. Just by listening this concerned human being restores life, gives hope, and often heals the broken-hearted. She'd never think of herself as the listening ear of God but I think she and all good people are precisely that.

I believe now that, seen and unseen, God is present to those who need God most.

A couple of weeks ago I visited a man in hospital. I knew he hadn't long to live and so did he. I just sat beside his bed and let him talk. When he asked me, I said a prayer and a blessing. He had a few questions which I answered as best I could but, I thought, without much conviction.

Next day he wrote me a little note. It said, 'Thanks for helping me to choose life in this time of uncertainty. I now know something wondrous is afoot. I just can't see it yet.' Two days later he died.

I had no idea how I helped him, but somehow he got the help to see death as 'something wondrous,' rather than something to be terrified of.

The artist Vincent Van Gogh said, 'God sends us works of art so that we can see ourselves in them.' He went on, 'The greatest artist of all is God who doesn't work on canvas, but with human flesh.'

I think that's a lovely thought. Even if my life is an abject failure, I am still a work of art in God's eyes.

A Gay man in our world

Here's a wonderful letter from a brave, articulate young man who has an issue he needs to speak about. I think he makes an unanswerable case. What do you think?

Father Brian,
I am a young member of an Irish parish. Until very recently I was involved in parish life and worked in church for the community. I enjoyed this involvement and it gave me great joy even though at times it was frustrating to see change happen so slowly.

I think I have a strong faith. This faith is based around the messages of Christ Jesus and I have a particular devotion to Our Lady. I feel that the clergy of the parish, and other members of the clergy that I have had dealings with, are a hard working and dedicated group of people who are all rich in faith and love of God. The reason why I'm writing to you is to try and explain why I have lost faith in my church.

The church is an organisation of believers that has grown over centuries into a massive structure with definite views and dogmas on various aspects of life. I am not welcome in the church that I have loved and worked hard for all my life. The reason why I feel I am not welcome is the fact that I am a gay man.

Believe me when I say that I did not choose this course in my life. It was chosen for me and I fought it for ten long hard years. I have broken hearts and have had my heart broken over the struggle I have had in accepting my sexuality. The church's views on this subject are clear to me and the rest of Irish society. It is these views that have me feeling angry every time I go to Mass. Hence the reason why I rarely go there anymore. I shouldn't feel angry or ashamed in the house of my Lord. I thought Mass was a celebration and a reminder of the sacrifice that was made for us. I think that my feelings of anger are not directed towards God but at the definite structure and organisation that is the Catholic Church.

Jesus said that those who were persecuted for seeking righteousness would have the kingdom of heaven. I have been persecuted for who I am, for what I believe and for what I think is right. Did Jesus mean me? Am I included in this beatitude?

I live with someone who loves me and I love him. The fact that he is a man does not change this love, it does not make it lesser nor greater, it just *is*. I thought that the commandment to love God and to love one another was to supersede all others, that from these would flow the other commandments. Maybe I am wrong in my thinking on this. Maybe the church is right. Maybe I am an abomination. What do you think? What does the church think and why on earth does it think this?

We do not leave children at the city gates for disobeying their parents, we do not stone to death adulterers and we do not scorn and shun those who work on Sundays. Why then does the church feel so strongly on certain people being allowed to love one another and certain others not being allowed to do so? I think that most of the discrimination, repulsion and sometimes hatred shown towards gay people in this country and in this parish is directly related to the views of the Catholic Church, my church.

I wonder if this letter might start a dialogue between us. I have prayed so strongly for faith because it has been pushed to its limits. I now pray for the church because it is being pushed to its limits and it still refuses to change. The people of the faith are infallible if they speak as one on matters of faith or doctrine. I'll bet if they were asked they would agree with me, let people love one another.

Hoping to hear from you soon. (Name used: John Doe)

Bill Gates' Rules of Life

Bill Gates gave a speech to young people. He taught them ten things they did not learn at school. They are relevant in these difficult times.

Rule 1: Life is not fair – get used to it!

Rule 2: The world won't care about your self esteem. The world will expect you to accomplish something *before* you feel good about yourself.

Rule 3: You will *not* make £50,000 a year right out of school. You won't be vice-president with a car until you earn both.

Rule 4: If you think your teacher is tough, wait until you get a boss.

Rule 5: Frying burgers is not beneath your dignity. Your grandparents had a different word for that; they called it opportunity.

Rule 6: If you mess up, it's not your parents' fault, so don't whine about your mistakes, learn from them.

Rule 7: Before you were born, your parents weren't as boring as they are now. They got that way from paying your bills, cleaning your clothes and listening to you talk about how cool you thought you were. So before you save the rain forest from the parasites of your parents' generation, try delousing the wardrobe in your own room.

Rule 8: Your school may have done away with winners and losers, but life has not. In some schools, they have abolished failing grades and they'll give you as many times as you want to get the right answer. This doesn't bear the slightest resemblance to anything in real life.

Rule 9: Life is not divided into terms. You don't get summers off and very few employers are interested in helping you find yourself. Do that in your own time.

Rule 10: Be nice to nerds. Chances are you'll end up working for one.

Forgiveness

To forgive those who have hurt us is one of the most difficult tasks in life. Yet not to forgive, is to give those who hurt us power to take away our peace. We should not give that power to any human being, so we must learn to forgive.

Resentment, jealously and bitterness are damaging emotions. Forgiveness is the only way to heal them.

Forgiveness is not a once off decision. It is a process and we have to keep working at it.

To begin to forgive the person who hurt us we must first recognise that we have been hurt.

Then we must admit our feelings of anger. In themselves feelings are neither right nor wrong. It's what we do with feelings that matters.

Next we have to trust somebody enough to share our feelings in a safe place. We can't cope with them in our own head. They will fester and wreck our peace if we do.

Not all forgiveness ends in reconciliation because it takes two be reconciled. If another person will not be reconciled, you can't give them power over your life. You have to move on. At some point when we decide to forgive, feelings of hurt and bitterness will linger on. Healing takes time.

There's a famous forgiveness prayer found in Auschwitz concentration camp which sums up forgiveness in practice:

Lord, remember not only people of goodwill,
but also people of ill will.
Do not remember only the sufferings
that have been afflicted on us,
but remember too the fruit we have bought,
as a result of this suffering
And when they come to judgement,
let all the fruits that we have borne be their forgiveness.

A helping hand

I got an e-mail just before Christmas with a message which was simple and direct: 'I have something to tell you. Ring me as soon as you can at one of the following numbers.'

I presumed this was just another rent-a-quote call from a journalist because the e-mail address was a national newspaper. I rang and she was delighted to hear from me.

'You don't know who I am Fr Brian, and you won't remember me, but you helped me 25 years ago when I needed help badly. I have been meaning to make this call for years but I decided not to let another Christmas go by without telling you.

'I wrote to you in 1982. My husband was an alcoholic and a brutal one at that. He walked out on us a couple of weeks before Christmas leaving me with a stack of bills and two young children under three to look after. You didn't know me. But you sent me a cheque which was enough to help pay the rent and get a few things for the children for Christmas. You helped me a few Christmases after that when I wrote to you, but we never met. I survived and you helped more than you know.

'The good news is that I've met another man who has been my saviour. We had two children of our own and when they got up a bit, I re-trained and went to work in this newspaper's office.

'The day after I got your cheque all those years ago I was walking the street with my two children when I found a £5 note fluttering in the breeze. I took it as a God-send.

'Now that I'm reasonably comfortable, myself and my husband have begun to drop money on the street hoping that somebody in need will find it. We scatter €50.00 a month, every month. We go to poor areas and let the money float in the breeze.

'That's all I wanted to tell you. You changed my life even though you didn't know it, and I hope our crazy way of scattering money will be a God send to those people who find it. Remember even a little help can and does go a long way.'

That's all she said. It was a lovely experience for me. Sometimes the past haunts us in a pleasing way!

What precisely is a good family?

That's a question I'm often asked. It's not an easy question to answer. Even the Holy Family of Jesus, Mary and Joseph had their problems. We get the impression they were holy and perfect in every way. Let's look at what the scriptures tell us about this 'perfect' family.

For one thing they couldn't have been that perfect because the mother and the father hadn't a sexual relationship.

When their child was born the father of the child was a mystery.

When the child was able to walk and think for himself he ran away from home as fast as he could. The parents had to go looking for him for three days and he was only 12 years old at this time. When the mother asked him where he was, he politely told her to mind her own business because he was about his 'father's business'. Mary and Joseph must have thought they were rearing a delinquent.

Jesus, right from the beginning, kept bad company. If he was the Messiah what was he doing with fishermen, shepherds, tax collectors and prostitutes? And then at the end of his life you'd think that the religious people would recognise him at least. But Messiah and Saviour meant nothing to them. They thought he was a fraud and a freak and wanted him put to death.

When he was dying his followers left him. His mother and a couple of women who were fond of him hung around and St John was there because he was too young to go anywhere else. And on his right and left hand were two criminals. He himself was condemned as a criminal. So if you are looking for a perfect family, I'm afraid the Holy Family is not the place to look.

I think that is great. Family life is hard work. As you can see, the Holy Family struggled. They had heartaches, fear, misunderstanding and doubt. But somehow they struggled through it. Jesus had compassion for people who were on the margins and who were hard done by. The only place he could have got that sympathy was from his family. So maybe the struggles and misunderstandings taught him to have love, compassion, forgiveness and acceptance that family is a safe place to be. That really is a good definition of a family. A place it's safe to be yourself. I wonder how many of our families are like that?

Here are a few tips I have picked up along the way. You can accept or reject them.

* Secrecy is the enemy of good relationships. Families are often more concerned about what the neighbours think than they are about the welfare of their own members. They put on a show. They'll keep difficulties quiet because they think it is bad to let them know the family's failings. Here's what secrecy does. It allows drunken men to beat up their wives. It allows children to be abused. It allows addicts, thugs and bullies to get away with it. Secrecy is the enemy of good relationships.

* Secondly, we don't have to be perfect. If you ever meet a perfect family run as quickly as you can in the opposite direction. Perfect families don't exist.

* You can't solve every problem. Mostly you can't solve your own problems, and you certainly can't solve problems for other people. There are some problems that are not solvable so don't waste your efforts on them.

* You don't have to fix people. It's not your job. Broken people quite often don't need fixing at all. If there is any fixing to be done they'll have to do it themselves.

Recently I attended a Golden Jubilee anniversary. The family got together and wrote a reflection which was their way of thanking their parents for what they gave them. This is part of their reflection:

Each of us will have our own special memories – maybe it's the rub of your beard, dad, when you got back from work; maybe it's licking the bowl, mum, after you made our birthday cakes. … As children we can sometimes take for granted the sacrifices that our parents make. As adults, however, we understand how your love for each other showed itself in the sheer hard work, and staying power, which is needed to sustain a marriage and to raise a family. You have risen to the challenges that 50 years can bring, the trials and triumphs alike. We love each of you for who you are, your personal qualities, your individual strengths of character, and everything you have given to us. You have made a marriage and a home, which nurtured us all and prepared us for life, wherever it would lead us.

If your children were your life's main work, then we hope that you are proud of your lives and our lives so far. You gave us something special, a shared set of values, a sense of family, the best education possible, the knowledge that hard work is nothing to fear and a belief in both doing our best and doing what's right. We thank you for all of those gifts.

Over the years you have offered a welcome to our friends and spouses who have so enriched our family circle. The life and love in our family has been truly multiplied by their presence. Mum and dad, we love you.

Wasn't it wonderful their parents heard those words while they were still alive.

Mystics and the future

Karl Rahner who, it could be argued, was the greatest theologian of the past one hundred years, repeatedly said that the Christians of tomorrow will either be mystics or they will be nothing at all.

He knew that all the unhealthy certainties of the past would disappear, forcing believers to discover the life and the love of God in the midst of their confused journey. For him the great love and the great suffering, which are essential parts of the mystic's way of life, open us to the unknowable.

Coincidently it was pointed out to me recently that the word 'mystic' is not even mentioned in the new *Catechism of the Catholic Church*. I checked, and 'mystic' doesn't appear in the Index of subjects anyway.

Those two statements tell us why we need healing in the church today. For the church as we know it, with its structures and hierarchy, the language of faith has become dogmatic and abstract; it speaks to the head and not the heart. Rahner's conviction about the mystics' search was that we have to slow down to find God; or, more precisely, be found by God, in all the places we never thought of looking. Faith for the mystic, is not so much about *what* we believe; faith is about *how* to believe.

How to believe in a changing world is what many of the articles in this collection are attempting to facilitate.

The criticism in that the official pronouncements of our church today don't relate to the world believers live in. It hasn't impinged upon many in leadership that religious practice is in decline and that the church as we knew it cannot be saved.

Vocations to priesthood and religious life are in freefall. Those priests who struggle on in ministry are overworked and elderly; too many are crippled by cold celibacy.

The church's edicts are meaningless and toothless and unsuited to the lives of people finding faith in new ways and in new places. We need a new way of being, to make faith relevant.

As long as we continue to live in denial we are not likely to accept God's Holy Spirit enlightening us. We will be trapped in tradition, unfree and unthinking.

True healing will begin when we allow our theologians the freedom to reflect, analyse, explore and teach. However, the theology which underpins this hierarchical church is incapable of dialogue with the modern world.

We need to kick-start reform by encouraging a theology which is based on the insight of the Second Vatican Council.

It was during the council that the Holy Spirit spoke with certainty and creativity. The problems which entomb us now are a direct result of the suppression of the Spirit of Vatican II. The cancer of clericalism has to be excised and an essential part of the treatment will be to affirm and encourage the church of the people of God.

Pastoral theology is in dire need of reform. Healing will begin when we welcome the infallibility of the praying people of God. That in turn will inevitably lead to a spiritual renewal. The mystics will be the prophets.

In the scriptures the prophet is a professional, inside, critic – a protected species. Today's church excommunicates the prophets.

In 1 Corinthians 12:28, St Paul lists prophecy as the second most important gift in the healing of a divided people. The early Christians believed healing began when there was a willingness to change.

We will never solve the problems of tomorrow by returning to the mistakes of the past. There is no alternative to the insights of the Second Vatican Council and there doesn't need to be, because that's where the Spirit lives.

Instead today's reactive church resorts to the theology of the ostrich, content to have a façade of unity and superficial respectability, which is nothing short of hypocrisy. We have replaced the morality of the gospel with the legalism of injunction about sex, contraception, homosexuality, divorce and celibacy.

We forget that people have matured and can think for themselves. They will not be treated like disobedient children.

'Respect' is a healing word. Respect for ourselves, respect for others – especially other churches. It is impossible to love our Catholic Church unless and until we appreciate the Spirit within every person who works sincerely for the spread of God's kingdom.

Ultimately healing can come only through the Spirit who

blows where she pleases to renew God's people. In Christ's plan the mission of those chosen to lead the church is to recognise, affirm, and enable the work of the Spirit to flourish in the community. That's what the Christian mystic must do – abandon everything, trusting God to lead us to a holy place.

10 major spiritual struggles of our age

Several years ago, the superior of the Missionary Oblates of Mary Immaculate in Rome asked Fr Ronald Rolheiser to compile a list of the major spiritual questions bubbling in the Catholic world, based on his experience as a writer and speaker. At the request of the *National Catholic Reporter,* Rolheiser recently took another look at that list, bringing it up to date in light of what he's seen and heard in the intervening period.

The following is the 'Top 10' list of major spiritual questions which we need to face, according to Rolheiser, and which I have summarised and paraphrased. I hope I do justice to the author.

1. The struggle with the atheism of our everyday consciousness, i.e. the struggle to have a vital sense of God within a secular world, to be a mystic rather than an unbeliever.
2. The struggle to live in torn, divided and highly polarised communities, as wounded persons ourselves, and carry that tension without resentment; to be healers and peacemakers rather than simply responding in kind.
3. The struggle to live, love and forgive beyond the ideologies we daily inhale, i.e. the struggle for true sincerity. To genuinely know and follow our own hearts and minds beyond what is prescribed to us by the right and the left. To be neither liberal nor conservative but rather men and women of true compassion.
4. The struggle to carry our sexuality without frigidity and without irresponsibility … to be both chaste and passionate.
5. The struggle for prayer in a culture which can't cope with depth and serenity – to keep our eyes set against an infinite horizon.
6. The struggle to cope with personal ambition and pathological restlessness, in a culture that daily over-stimulates them … to accept that in this life there is no finished symphony.
7. The struggle not to be motivated by paranoia, fear, narrowness and over protectionism in the face of terrorism and overpowering complexity; not to let the need for clarity and security destroy compassion and truth.

8. The struggle with moral loneliness inside a religious, cultural, political and moral diaspora, to find a soul mate who sleeps with us at our deepest level.
9. The struggle to link faith to justice, ecology, and gender – to have a letter of reference from the poor.
10. The struggle to find the healthy line between individuality and community, spirituality and ecclesiology, to be both mature and committed, spiritual and ecclesial.

These are good principles to discuss deeply and sincerely if we are to be human and spiritual searchers. True healing always sets us off on the spiritual search for meaning.